Preparing Teachers
as
Professionals

The Role of Educational Studies and
Other Liberal Disciplines

LANDON E. BEYER
WALTER FEINBERG
JO ANNE PAGANO
JAMES ANTHONY WHITSON

TEACHERS
COLLEGE
PRESS

Teachers College, Columbia University
New York and London

Published by Teachers College Press, 1234 Amsterdam Avenue
New York, NY 10027

Library of Congress Cataloging-in-Publication Data

Preparing teachers as professionals: the role of educational studies
    and other liberal disciplines/Landon E. Beyer . . . [et al.].
        p. cm.
    Includes bibliographical references.
    ISBN 0-8077-2989-2.—ISBN 0-8077-2988-4 (pbk.)
    1. Teachers—Training of—United States.   2. Education—Study and
teaching—United States.   I. Beyer, Landon E., 1949–
LB1715.P73 1989   89-37677
370'.71'0973—dc20   CIP

Manufactured in the United States of America

96 95 94 93 92 91 90 89   8 7 6 5 4 3 2 1

Contents

Introduction

The development of approaches to education, including the founding of public schools and the creation of institutions for the preparation of teachers, did not arise independently of the social, political, and economic patterns present in the wider society. Some indication of the historical precedents affecting contemporary educational debates is important if we are to understand how larger contexts continue to affect the outcome of those debates. Of particular importance are the ties between schools and teacher-training institutions, and the dynamics of social class, gender, and race/ethnicity that have shaped education and the profession of teaching in ways that further a functional relationship between education and larger social structures.

The eventual direction of our educational institutions was affected by a number of interlocking ideas and values that were central to those who advocated public education. Educational proposals such as those of Thomas Jefferson in the eighteenth century saw institutions of public education not only as places for pupils and prospective teachers to receive intellectual stimulation but also as central means for ensuring social progress and the perfection of humankind. Such an Enlightenment view dovetailed with the American emphasis on democracy and republican institutions, since schools might focus on fostering the literacy and civic awareness that is presumably required for the political participation of all citizens. The establishment of democratic rule entailed the establishment of education for all. The belief in both progress and the perfectibility of people through the manipulation of social institutions, combined with a commitment to popular governance, produced a view of American society in which moral virtue, democratic institutions, and popular education went hand in hand.

These central beliefs were perceptively noted by Tocqueville in his visits to this country in the 1830s. Tocqueville also recognized another facet of the American character: a commitment to activism and a kind of social and institutional "pragmatism" (in the vulgar sense of that term). At its most virulent, this American activism resulted in an anti-intellectualism and a suspicion of any form of theoretical reflection; rather, immediate responses to current predicaments were favored. As Tocqueville commented:

> Men who live in democratic communities not only seldom indulge in meditation, but they naturally entertain very little esteem for it. . . . The man of action . . . has occasion perpetually to rely on ideas that he has not had leisure to search to the bottom; for he is much more frequently aided by the seasonableness of an idea than by its strict accuracy . . . a rapid glance at particular incidents, the daily study of the fleeting passions of the multitude, the accidents of the moment, and the art of turning them to account decide all its affairs. (cited in Borrowman, 1956, p. 32)

An emphasis on "pragmatic" action, perhaps even at the expense of reflection and a full consideration of alternatives, was to have a signal influence on the development of education and teaching in the United States.

Also central to the worldview affecting the nineteenth-century educational reformer was a commitment to individualism and self-reliance. America was to provide opportunities to individuals whose hard work, diligence, and thrift could alter their stations in life. Thus one of the central lessons to be taught in any reformed system of schooling was that hard work and fair competition would allow citizens the opportunity to succeed and prosper within a growing social and economic order. Yet a central ambiguity in American social life is here manifested: the tension between what Bellah, Madsen, Sullivan, Swidler, and Tipton (1985) call "self-reliant competitive enterprise and a sense of public solidarity" (p. 256). In a fundamental sense this tension has its origins in the contrast between the equality, community, and participation fostered in our democratic rhetoric and the competitive, nonegalitarian, and individualistic nature of economic practices in a capitalistic society.

The existence of social-class, gender, and racial/ethnic inequalities was exacerbated by the influx of immigrant groups, the members of which often became victims of this stratification. Factories employing large numbers of unskilled and semiskilled workers—immigrants as well as established Americans from the lower class—made more pronounced the inequalities already present in U.S. society. Possessing customs, languages, and political and religious beliefs that were often unfamiliar to settled Americans, immigrants evoked apprehension on the part of many, including the early proponents of public education (Nasaw, 1979).

The inequalities in American society became more and more obvious as our cities grew. This stratification could be seen not only in economic organizations like the newly emerging textile mills in New England, but in cultural and educational practices as well. Despite the touting of equality, opportunity, and the benefits of hard work by government and educational leaders, higher education in the United States took place almost exclusively in private academies and colleges, where only the economically privileged could afford to send their sons. Women were generally not admitted, at least on an equal basis, to institutions of higher education, just as blacks were generally excluded from publicly supported institutions of education. This pattern of gender, social-class, and racial inequality was to have a decided impact on the nature of schooling and the profession of teaching in this country, affecting both the teacher workforce and the ideas and ideologies of the classroom. The effects of social inequality were especially pronounced within programs created to prepare future teachers.

Before the development of normal schools in the 1840s, teachers' institutes had been organized. Reflecting the religious orientation of the nineteenth-century schoolpeople, these early "inservice workshops" were more like revival meetings than intellectual gatherings. The stress was on the moral integrity of teachers, as their character was considered the primary variable in teaching success or failure. The teachers' institute was the major force for "preparing young men for a worthy profession in education . . . [and] for 'awakening' aspirant professionals" (Mattingly, 1975, p. 62). As with other "revival meetings," women attended but could not participate in the teachers' institutes, where those present would be "filled with the spirit," "called," and "awakened" to the moral nature of teaching. "Most of all, the institute, like the revival, proposed to transform a congregation of individuals into a conscious moral body with its own special tone and spiritual goal, the two essential elements of awakening and professionalization" (Mattingly, 1975, p. 67). Later these institutes took greater responsibility for developing standards for the profession; instead of focusing on the moral awakening and personal character of the teacher, they concentrated more on technical skills and practical training.

The American Institute of Instruction (AII), founded in 1830, offered a different emphasis for the preparation of teachers. Members of this organization favored college graduation as a prerequisite for teaching, so that practicing teachers would be scholars as well as schoolkeepers. Yet implementing such an ideal was problematic. For one thing, teachers were drawn largely from the working class, whose families could not afford the expense of higher education in private academies and universities; for another, most of the candidates were women. The education such students had themselves received in grammar schools was often rather cursory, so that those responsible for preparing teachers often faced the task of remedial instruction.

The need to draw from those whose education could not be taken for granted, and who were cut off from other occupational pursuits, exemplifies one of the central tensions in the profession of teaching. The prestigious eastern colleges, offering programs and courses in the traditional liberal arts, all but excluded students whose educational and economic backgrounds (and in practice, of course, these two are highly correlated) left them insufficiently prepared for such a course of study. At the same time, the traditional liberal arts colleges almost always refused to recognize education as a legitimate area of study, at least through the Civil War period (and, for some, to this day). The opportunity of pursuing a teaching career was characteristically seized by those people excluded from the elite higher education establishment. This reflected the social-class distinctions that were realities of American economic life, even as they coexisted with more egalitarian political rhetoric.

While many teachers looked for practical guidance through techniques of instruction rather than for philosophical reflection on their activities, the emphasis on moral values and character remained a key ingredient of teacher preparation. However, it was a peculiarly apolitical and asocial morality that was to dominate. Contentious people and contentious ideas were equally unwelcome in public educational institutions that taught the common virtues in a way that would guarantee social harmony and self-reliance within a changing social and economic order.

One of the principal figures advocating both common schools and a system of teacher preparation was Horace Mann, appointed first Secretary of the Massachusetts Board of Education in 1837. Fearing the disruptions of social change that were taking place in Europe and elsewhere, Mann advocated the creation of a common ground through schooling that would defuse political and even intellectual conflict. As he said in his twelfth and final report to the Massachusetts Board of Education, in 1848:

> If the tempest of political strife were to be let loose upon our Common Schools, they would be overwhelmed with sudden ruin. . . . A preliminary advantage, indispensable to ultimate success, will be the appointment of a teacher of the true faith. (cited in Cremin, 1957, pp. 94–95)

Mann's faith in the public schools reflects his enlightenment zeal, for he saw the schools as the primary means of social progress and individual well-being.

> "Never will wisdom preside in the halls of legislation," [Mann] wrote, "and its profound utterances be recorded on the pages of the statute book, until Common Schools . . . shall create a more far-seeing intelligence and a purer morality than has ever existed among communities of men." (Cremin, 1957, p. 7)

Throughout the nineteenth century, there was never a clean break between the schoolhouse and the various institutions and agencies responsible for preparing teachers. Mann's crusade for normal schools was as enthusiastic as his advocacy of the common school. Normal schools, Mann claimed, have historic importance, since they form "a new instrumentality of the race. . . . Neither the art of printing, nor the trial by jury, nor a free press, nor a free suffrage can long exist to any beneficial and salutary purpose without schools for the training of teachers" (cited in Richardson, 1900, p. 12).

Yet the spread of normal schools was far from rapid. In 1860 there were only 11 state-appointed institutions in existence, and graduates made little impact on the profession as a whole. Their numbers increased after the Civil War, so that by 1898, 167 normal schools were in operation (Elsbree, 1939). The graduates of these schools still played a minor role in developing the profession, however, in part because normal schools could not meet the need for new teachers that was being felt at the turn of the century. This heightened demand was largely due to the increase in public school attendance, spurred both by a growing industrial technology that required advanced training for employees and by an enforcement of truancy laws for students.

Summarizing the first century of normal school education, Charles A. Harper (1939) clarified one of the dimensions of the divergence between normal schools and colleges. At least the second generation of normal school advocates saw the preparation of teachers in predominantly functional terms. Just as normal schools were created out of the climate that fostered common schools, their direction was taken from educational needs as defined by those schools and the communities within which they existed. This allowed for regional and even local autonomy, especially early on, as normal schools developed to meet the varying conditions and aims of their constituencies. Yet this reliance on local values and expectations also resulted in the closer replication of whatever social and educational inadequacies might manifest themselves within these largely rural and somewhat provincial communities.

In discussing the view of education the prospective teacher must have, David P. Page (1847) advocated a blend of mental discipline and moral training, asserting that "the love of moral truth should be as early addressed as the love of knowledge" (p. 71). He spoke often of the broad range of duties confronting the teacher, including responsibilities for children's bodily health (together with students' parents), intellectual growth (including the proper order of study, the manner of study, and collateral study), moral training (mainly by example, flowing from the "purity of soul" of the teacher), and religious training. Much of this responsibility was to be discharged not in didactic instruction of subject matter, but through the habits, demeanor, and spirit of teachers themselves. The necessity of inculcating the proper values and attitudes resulted in the development of a set of dispositional guides for students that only later would be incorporated into a hidden curriculum—at this juncture they were quite intentional and overt (Vallance, 1977).

Within normal school programs, "fitting in" to social and community expectations was the key educational value. It was a similar set of commitments that led Horace Mann to abhor the inclusion of controversial ideas within the common school curriculum. Both types of educational institutions placed a premium on avoiding interpersonal and political strife and on facilitating social harmony.

As normal schools gained in popularity and attendance, the bifurcation of college education and normal school training intensified. Only in 1894, for example, did Massachusetts require a high school diploma for admission to normal schools (Harper, 1939); still, by 1900 high school graduation was seldom a requirement for admission. It was not until 1930 that a high school diploma became a common entrance requirement for normal school students (Elsbree, 1939). Thus the status of teaching as a profession was in question as normal schools aligned themselves with traditions that separated them from a substantial portion of their own roots—as exemplified by the earlier American Institute of Instruction—as well as from other professions and educational institutions. Referring to the students who would fill the classrooms of the normal school, W. F. Phelps of the Winona, Minnesota, Normal School contended that, "however important to society the liberally *educated* man may be, it is of greater importance still that the industrial classes in this country should become the recipients of a *training* befitting their condition and their weighty responsibilities" (American Normal School, 1871, p. 15; emphasis added).

The social-class, gender, and racial/ethnic influences on the normal schools were directly related to the sort of education being offered in the common school. Since the public elementary schools were occupied with the instruction of working-class pupils and immigrant children who needed to be "Americanized," the curriculum often reflected the expectations held for these students. For instance, one writer advocated the inclusion of the natural sciences "in their relations to agriculture and the mechanic arts" for the elementary student, since "these are studies of the first importance *to the industrial classes,* and as far as possible they ought either to accompany or supplement thorough instruction in the so-called common branches" (American Normal School, 1871, p. 16; emphasis added). The social-class origin and probable destination of common school students affected their early curricular experiences, just as normal school training was shaped in accord with the social-class backgrounds of students.

The distinction between the appropriate course of study for normal school students and that for college enrollees was rather sharply drawn. The distinction was based on the quality of primary education that the working or industrial classes enjoyed, on a certain contempt on the part of the second generation of normal school advocates for the classical curriculum of the liberal arts college, and on a repudiation of professional studies by faculties in the liberal arts. Students of the liberal arts might be content to study languages and literature, periods of history, and elocutionary styles, for example; yet for a working-class normal school student, these had little professional utility.

The course of study for prospective teachers was thus linked to the social-class backgrounds of normal school students and the expectations of the communities served by the common schools. It was, therefore, to be limited and well focused. The principal of the State Normal School of West Virginia argued, for instance, that:

> As long as teachers are required to study a great deal more than they are expected to teach, the mass of teachers for the elementary schools will not go into the normal schools, and consequently will not receive that professional instruction . . . which every one feels so necessary to the highest success. (American Normal School, 1871, p. 23)

Combined with both an emphasis on practical coursework rather than "speculative dreams" and an apprenticeship approach to professional development, the normal school oriented students toward the current "nonpartisan," "apolitical" realities of teaching. Rejecting both the scholar's dispassionate search for truth and the nonuseful studies of the private liberal arts colleges, the normal school organizers created a system of training that emphasized adaptation, predictability, replication, nondivisiveness, and a narrow, utilitarian selection of subject matter. Moreover, the fact that teaching became, in the words of Catharine Beecher, "the true and noble profession of a woman" (cited in Hoffman, 1981, p. 4) was to have a decided impact on schooling and teacher preparation.

Criticizing the lack of cooperation among teachers of different subjects and grades, as well as the lack of freedom for individual teachers, Ella Flagg Young (1901) saw the routine and drudgery of schoolteaching as closely related to the technicalization of normal school training and to the overemphasis on the supervision of women teachers by male administrators. Further, as teacher training increasingly emphasized the incidentals of teaching at the expense of a more liberal education, Young (1901) perceived other results as well:

This subjection to drudgery was compensated for by the introduction of the terms "faithful" and "conscientious" as applicable to those who devoted themselves to perfecting the dull
routine. What was the influence of this magnification of
drudgery upon the personnel of the teaching corps? This question brings forward the subject of the remarkable decrease in
the number of men teachers, and corresponding increase in the
number of women teachers, in city elementary schools.
(pp. 39–40)

The unequal opportunities afforded men in fields like medicine, law, science, business, and the ministry, of course, greatly
affected the gender specificity of the teaching force. Yet the lack
of autonomy enjoyed by teachers is also dynamically linked to the
gender realities of the profession. The tedium and loss of individ-
uality that tended to accompany the bureaucratized, routinized
elementary classroom, and the narrow normal school training
that provided the route to those classrooms, were realities that
influenced occupational selection by gender. The nature of
teacher-training programs as well as the working conditions of
elementary schools were reciprocally related to the subjugation
of women and the reality of patriarchal modes of control in
schools and the wider society.

Yet not all teacher-preparation practices, nor all public school
classrooms, reflected these gender-specific conditions in such
stark terms. Many women worked long hours, for little pay, in
adverse circumstances to educate the youth of the expanding
United States. Their stories are poetic testimony to the sense of
social mission and personal possibility that teaching provided (see
Hoffman, 1981; Snyder, 1972). In pointing to the inequalities of
American social life that affected the work of teachers and their
professional preparation, it is important to place these in the
context of the real lives of women, for whom teaching offered a
chance not only to earn a living but also to achieve a limited form
of autonomy and a sense of purpose. The profession of teaching,
then as now, was framed by contradictions—"less than equal in
status to male professions, *and* a source of satisfaction and power
for women" (Hoffman, 1981, pp. 15–16).

Teaching was, for Beecher and others, more than just a way
of extending the culture of domesticity through moral and religious evangelism in the growing number of common schools. It
also provided women a concrete alternative to marriage and fac-

tory work. If teaching could be made an honorable profession, and the teacher a respected member of the community in which the school was located, an option would be created that would have positive material and social consequences (though teachers, to be true to Beecher's view that their sole purpose is to "do good," must not enter the profession because of those consequences). The adverse conditions of employment for most women in the cities, where they often worked for less than subsistence wages, in dirty, unhealthy, stressful environments, made it especially important that women create professional alternatives. And schoolteaching offered just such an alternative, even as it drew upon women's "natural" gifts and instincts.

The view that schoolteaching was a natural choice for women was widely shared, in spite of the fact that teaching had originally been dominated by men seeking temporary employment. The expectations for common school teachers were directly tied to the fact that teaching had become a distinctly woman's profession, dominated by a nurturant rather than an academic orientation. Professor W. E. Crosby, of Iowa, expressed sentiments that were common before and long after his time:

> Every woman of this land, should be a successful teacher; should be able to teach. Now, every young lady that enters a high school should be able to train children; and the one who is prepared for that work of teaching in the school, is all the better prepared for the duties of life. (American Normal School, 1871, p. 25)

Since the "duties of life" for "homemakers" were not far removed from the nurturant duties of the schoolteacher, the completion of normal school training by women might well be perceived as appropriate preparation for adulthood.

With the advent of the common school, and increasing with the beginning of the Civil War, teaching became more and more dominated by women. For the four decades beginning in 1840, the number of women teachers tripled, so that by 1880 they constituted 80 percent of the teachers in the common schools (Hoffman, 1981). This increase was partially due to the war itself, since young men who might otherwise have become teachers were sent off to fight. Yet more important than this were the increased job opportunities in the expanding industrial cities of the Northeast and, later on, the Midwest. The expansion of capitalism meant jobs in the factories for males; thus more and more teaching vacancies were filled by women whose employment prospects and opportunities for higher education were severely limited. As has been the case with other professions, when teaching became unattractive to men and "women's work," its status declined.

Teaching was undertaken in large numbers by women who received one-half to one-third of the salary of men, who were to be "called" to the profession because of their commitment to "do good" rather than because of any monetary or status rewards that might accrue to them. As men prepared for the more lucrative professions in the public sphere, the classroom, like the household, became the sphere of the private, the domestic. The separation of personal and public, reason and emotion, head and heart—entrenched in societies such as ours that foster unequal gender relations—had a decided impact on the nature of teaching and the preparation of schoolteachers.

This brief history of some of our central educational ideas and institutions indicates the intricate relation of education to the society within which it exists and to the dynamics of social inequality in the United States (Feinberg, 1983). Especially important here are the dynamics of social class, gender, and race/ethnicity that permeated the educational policies of both the public schools and institutions for the preparation of teachers. The interest in creating people and programs that would be uncontentious, apolitical, and functionally related to social expectations affected the practice of teaching and the development of school curricula. What is perhaps most remarkable about this history is the extent to which a disavowal of or inattention to perhaps unpleasant social realities has helped cement educational ideas and practices to those very forces. This is perhaps clearest at times of proposed educational change—a point that should be clear from the reform effort of the 1980s.

Yet visions of alternative social and educational ideas and practices have also been present throughout our history. Some of these have enjoyed at least partial success from time to time and are insightful in providing alternatives as we reflect on the contemporary situation in which we find ourselves. In addition, the moral dimensions of teaching—even if only partially disclosed during historical attempts at reform—are central issues as we rethink the nature of education and teaching. A moral commitment to "do good" is one that may profitably be reclaimed.

CHAPTER 1

Educational Studies and Liberal Learning

This is a book about education—the study of education and its practices. It is also a book about teacher education. One of its central themes is that teacher education is not so far removed from liberal education as present-day reformers seem to suppose, that teacher education conceived outside of a technocratic framework may serve as a model for what we are pleased to call liberal education. We choose the word *theme* to designate the center of our text because of its etymological association with action as well as with discourse. Teacher education, we shall argue, ought to contain among its goals the emancipation of mind and spirit and the disposition to action that ought to inform any "education" in a democracy. This project will involve a redefinition of terms commonly invoked in discussions of the liberal arts and of professional study. Among these are the terms *the liberal arts* and *profession* themselves. As might be expected, then, we shall take particular care to explore, in the various registers in which our theme is played, the elements of knowing and acting, content and method, and theory and practice. The character and force of the educational work that results depends on how these elements are arranged.

THE CONTEMPORARY "CRISIS" IN EDUCATION

We are, we are told, currently in a state of educational crisis. Since the announcement of this crisis in *A Nation at Risk* (The

National Commission on Excellence in Education, 1983), government officials, business and community leaders, educational researchers, and intellectuals and academicians of all stripes have taken up positions on education; many have focused their interest on teacher education, believing it to be the root of all evil. Since 1983, a number of reports assessing the quality and status of public education and drawing implications for teacher education have appeared. These have been taken up energetically by a public eager to get a handle on the endemic anxiety that contemporary cultural critics report as a condition of life in a postmodern, postindustrial world. This is not surprising. The same fears, anxieties, and social interests that provoked the common school movement during the 1840s and the secondary school movement at the end of the nineteenth century are very much present today. These are fears of social disintegration, fears of assault on those values and habits of life that must be possessed in common by all citizens if democratic structures are to be maintained. And like our progressive nineteenth-century forebears, we continue to place our faith in the possibility of a future in which universal public education inculcates values and goals conducing toward a *public* good.

There is a great deal of overlap between the thinking of nineteenth-century reformers and present-day critics. Much of the language urging reform is the same, and many of the reform proposals in their gross aspects appear similar. In fact, a great deal of nineteenth-century common sense persists in academic as well as in popular thinking about education today. *A Nation at Risk* in particular, with its pointed appeals to a moral rectitude expressed through discipline and hard work and revealed in economic superiority, is redolent of the nineteenth-century combination of nostalgia for preindustrial pastoral community and fear of the unknown forces unleashed by technology and industry. And like nineteenth-century thinkers, the framers of the presidential commission's report and other proposals find cause for optimism in the progress promised by a scientific approach to the social world. But there are important differences, and these are most pronounced in the proposals of the Carnegie Forum on Education and the Economy (1986) and the Holmes Group (1986). These two documents direct their concern and effort toward the professionalization of teaching, and by *professionalization* they mean something that only began to have meaning during the nineteenth century and that then had few of the ramifications the term now has.

When the Carnegie Forum on Education and the Economy (1986) urges steps toward professionalization of teachers and teacher educators, they have in mind some very specific moves. These include organizing teaching hierarchically, such that one's progress through one's professional life is marked by increments in responsibilities and rewards, such increments presumably reflecting attainment of increasing skill and professional refinement. Also included are recommendations for monitoring both student achievement and teacher productivity. For our purposes, the two most important features of the Carnegie proposal are the recommendations that a National Board for Professional Teaching Standards be constituted and that all prospective teachers complete a four-year program of study in a department of the arts and sciences prior to beginning professional study in a program of teacher preparation. The National Board would act as a certifying agency guaranteeing the "competency" of teachers. Not only would it regulate entry into the profession, it would also regulate progress through the profession as well as specify the form and content of teacher-preparation programs. A prerequisite to Board certification would be a "master of teaching" degree earned through a program emphasizing field experiences integrated with professional coursework to develop skills in instruction and management.

The most comprehensive and influential document dealing with the specifics of teacher preparation has been the Holmes Group (1986) report, *Tomorrow's Teachers*. This report must be read as at least partially motivated by the concern of its authors to ensure their continued presence in the academy. That this document should have appeared at a time during which the necessity and value of professional preparation for teaching are being questioned is no coincidence. The Holmes Group has responded to attacks on teacher preparation by trying to safeguard to teacher educators an area of expertise not shared by their liberal arts colleagues. The 17 deans of "prestigious" schools of education who framed the report share the common-sense notions of education and teacher preparation that have made earlier reports so compelling to academics and the general public alike. It is this appeal to common sense that permits the Holmes report to be assimilated to the rhetoric of school criticism, thereby insuring it a positive reception even as it contests the common-sense view that studies in education are without value. The notions of education with which we will be concerned here may even be defining characteristics of the American psyche.

In common-sense thinking, there are two kinds of knowledge: knowledge that is good in itself but, curiously, *good-for-nothing*, and knowledge that is good-for-something but worthless in itself (cf., e.g., Hamerow, 1987, pp. 28–29). This distinction finds parallels in a number of other distinctions—that between knowing and acting, judging and acting, being and doing, and so forth. It is related to Ryle's (1949) intuitively appealing distinction between "knowing-that" and "knowing-how." It is related to the distinction between study *in* the liberal arts and study *for* the professions, a distinction expressed concretely in the bifurcation of content and methodology. One of the arguments we shall make is that those distinctions have a lot of soft edges. Ours is a Wittgensteinian view of mastery, one in which knowing anything at all is seen as "knowing-how-and-that" (see Cavell, 1979; Morawetz, 1978).

Like the Carnegie and other recommendations, the Holmes report presumes that improving the quality of teaching will result necessarily in improving the quality of education. Like many other reports, the Holmes document also presumes that we know what we mean and are all agreed on what improved teaching and improved education would be like. Usually these are reduced to student learning as assessed by some sort of standardized performance measure. And like the others, the Holmes report also recommends a hierarchically structured and strictly controlled profession. The teachers who are at the top of the professional hierarchy will be those who, in addition to mastery of a traditional liberal arts and sciences discipline, are in control of a body of knowledge about learning and development. The academic major is good-in-itself but good-for-nothing; it is, however, a necessary *foundation* for the study of teaching, a study that will prepare teachers to transmit the good-in-itself to future generations of learners. Such study, according to the Holmes Group, must be study of a body of knowledge unique to the practice of teaching. That body of knowledge is to be selected from among the behavioral sciences, again expressing the distinction between knowing and doing that would situate knowledge and action in wholly different fields. Here content and method are neatly severed, to be joined later in an instrumental relationship.

While such a conceptional relationship might appear logical, it is not sensible. Let us take, for example, language acquisition as a paradigm of learning. It is obvious that one learns to do a great many things with a language before one can say anything *about* it. And when the moment is achieved when we can speak *about* our language, we simultaneously begin to *do* a great many other things with it. Among those things that we may do is teach that language—an act that requires the use of the language.

If we view entry into a profession as involving processes similar to those involved in the process of initiation into a linguistic community, then some objects on the horizon of the standard way of viewing seem very odd. First, it seems strange to conceive of content as foundational to practice. When we teach, we teach *something*—something handled and employed in the act of teaching. The characteristics or features of what is taught affect how it is to be taught, so that what we teach itself helps define the activity of teaching; again, the activities of teaching give shape to what is taught, giving life to that content. Neither content nor practice can be seen as foundational, since they exist in reciprocal relationships whereby each has a role in defining the other.

We are distressed by the invisibility in all of the reports and recommendations of those dimensions that we consider crucial to the act of teaching, or indeed to the practice of any profession. Most attempts to redefine teacher preparation stress a narrow conception of teacher professionalization. Since the nineteenth century, the persistent curriculum problem in the university has been that of the relationship between professional and liberal education. And there has existed an enduring tension, amounting often to hostility, between liberal arts and professional faculties within the university. At many elite liberal arts colleges, the continued existence of education departments has often been imperiled by a conviction that teaching is a trade. Many of the current proposals, and probably in particular the Holmes report (1986), must be read as responses to that threat. While it is not always clear what professionalization implies, at least a few assumptions seem to recur with some regularity. All of these are concerned chiefly with upgrading the status and respectability of the profession.

The first common assumption is that naming and legitimating a body of knowledge can serve as an adequate foundation of educational study. The Holmes Group (1986) finds this foundational knowledge in the behavioral sciences. The pervasive tendency toward technocracy that underlies this recommendation makes an unintuitive and unsubstantiated necessary connection between science and the latest in a series of educational slogans: "educational excellence." Of course, it all depends on what one means by "excellence," but that is not a topic considered in such literature. It is a central issue in this book. In most of the literature under discussion, excellence, in education and in teaching, is clearly indicated by measurable student achievement. That being the case, the behavioral sciences appear to be the logical choice of a body of knowledge to form the core of professional studies, if, indeed, achievement is defined in behavioral terms. We shall argue, as did Nyberg and Egan (1984) and Gowin (1981), that educational practice requires a theory of education and that a theory of education cannot be assimilated to theories of psychology or learning because of the ethical and political dimensions of teaching. We shall also argue that teaching and learning are not symmetrical.

Another recurrent assumption is that time spent in study of education and pedagogy is time that interferes with the student's real—that is, liberal—education. The liberal arts are to provide content that can then be utilized in the methodology-oriented professional study in education. "Teaching" thus comes to mean the transmission of liberal knowledge through appropriate professional means. Finally, while liberal and professional study are both seen as important, their importance involves extending the time spent on each, thereby ensuring their continued separation. The bifurcation of liberal and professional studies, however, rests on a mistake regarding the nature of practice, a mistake having extensive educational and professional ramifications. The sense of profession dominating discourse on teacher preparation since the appearance of such influential books as Lortie's *Schoolteacher* (1975) and Jackson's *Life in Classrooms* (1968) owes everything to Parsons's general structural-functionalist account of social arrangements. The Parsonian story of society has long been incorporated into the organization, both administrative and conceptual, of our schools at all levels—from elementary through graduate. The danger in reconceptualizing the profession of teaching from this perspective is that teaching and learning will finally come to be rationalized solely as technical production processes. Central to our project in this book is developing a notion of practice in which liberal and professional studies are part of the same existential project, a notion of practice that does not hang it on the coattails of theory, and a notion of practice in which it is at once foundational and derivative.

EDUCATIONAL REFORM AND PRIOR QUESTIONS

This volume is concerned with questions that are prior to those currently asked by many educational reformers. These questions concern the nature of the professions, of liberal knowledge, of teaching, and of the institutional contexts in which all of these occur. They are questions that must be raised if more specific issues are to be resolved intelligently.

For example, consider the quest for an appropriate, guiding body of knowledge for teacher-preparation programs and practices. Rather than assuming the necessity of some such body of knowledge, we wish to ask a number of critical questions about the assumptions built into this quest. One such question is why, and under what circumstances, people might seek such guiding or regulative ideas. It is useful to authenticate such a body of knowledge when the professions are conceived in a particular, and rather problematic, way. Such a body of knowledge is generally sought when we assume a field is characterized by a logic of technical application, where decisions about actions are based on a set of guiding principles. Yet if such a set of principles forms the knowledge that guides decision making in specific, practical situations, what is required is knowing when and how to undertake the necessary steps to bring practice into conformity with those rules. Indeed, a "body of knowledge," especially of a scientific kind, is often thought essential precisely because it can provide definitive directions to practice and guarantee proper results. But what if teaching requires something more than technical rationality and something more than subject-matter expertise? What other ways are there to conceptualize teaching, and in what ways do teachers actually practice their craft? If we knew these things, in what ways might we characterize the profession? What difference would all of this make to how we go about preparing teachers? Finally, how would this alter our view of educational studies? We investigate the possibilities contained in these questions against the background of a critically grounded conception of liberal inquiry, arguing finally that teaching itself is a form of liberal inquiry and that educational studies are liberal studies.

Our view is that the development of educational studies as a professional domain requiring technical rationality (Habermas, 1971) has been injurious to patterns of schooling and teaching. Advocates of technical rationality have substituted its requirements and desires—the requirements and desires of hierarchical,

patriarchal, bureaucratic institutions—for the humane requirements of the profession of teaching. Technical rationality as
applied to education has resulted in denigrating and devalorizing
the dimensions of practice and judgment that characterize teaching at its best and most committed. It is an expression of the kind
of logocentric thinking criticized by Derrida (1976), among others, that results in such binary oppositions as theory/practice and
liberal/applied. It has also served to obscure and distort the ethical, political, and ideological imperatives specific to educational
practice by its pretension to scientific objectivity (Beyer, 1988a).
If teaching involves primarily the articulation of practices that
further preestablished outcomes, if desire is satisfied by meeting
standards of efficiency and predictability, the political nature of
curriculum decisions, for example, is hidden. A commitment to
technical rationality and to a body of decontextualized knowledge
as a guide to practice serves an important social function. The
socially and politically interested nature of our knowledge and
practice are safe from criticism.

For example, consider the ways in which curriculum decisions are frequently made in schools. Given the dominant efficiency orientation of the field, and the constraints on teaching
when it is conceived as enhancing students' scores on standardized tests, we are led to see curriculum deliberation in quantifi-
able, technical terms. The focus of such deliberation is frequently
on how a program, textbook, or set of materials will accomplish
an end that has been identified—for example, the extent to which
high school students will increase their scores on the ACT exams,
or the degree to which a basal reading series can increase the
reading level of elementary school pupils. Lost in such decisions is
the realization that the selection of content for the curriculum, as
well as the forms in which it is presented and the means by which
it is evaluated, often involve complex, difficult political and moral
questions (Beyer & Apple, 1988). Questions such as whose
knowledge is included and excluded, or how these decisions affect
larger social and cultural practices, are not verbalized when our
commitments are to the technical manipulation of a decontextualized, presumably objective, body of knowledge.

In the sciences, a view of objective inquiry is sometimes
expressed in the conviction that the "context of discovery" of an
empirical circumstance is logically separable from the "logic of
justification." What is central here is the conviction that we
arrive at demonstrable truths in ways that can be objectively

ascertained and conclusively, or nearly conclusively, demonstrated. Even in philosophical analysis, many have alleged that clarifying our conceptual structures does not necessitate any awareness of the concrete contexts out of which they may have arisen; indeed, such exploration is often considered irrelevant. So too, liberal disciplines often promise just such transcendence in their nostalgia for a past that never was—a rule of the One of Reason over the Opinion of the Many.

There are, of course, others who would have us consider teaching as an art form. In fact, some of the most compelling and literate writing on teaching is by those who have judged their teachers to be artists. Education in this view, rather than being something to be got or had, is experienced, and the experience is an aesthetic one. Let us consider the consequences of such a view. If teaching is conceived and practiced as an art form, it would include investigation of specific traditions, styles, and techniques, to be sure. But no set of abstract rules could guide practice, and practice and judgment would keep messing up prediction and expectation. Instead, the actual act of teaching would become central to working out the meaning of teaching, just as the placing of the paint on the canvas is central to the significance of the painting. The act and its object fuse in practice. We might, of course, ask the artist to tell about ideas, decisions, choices in technique and style, but these are part of the work. Technical rationality applied to teaching, in the artistic view, is like painting by numbers. An artistic object or act is not one that can be reduced to its technical aspect, although technique serves such objects and acts. What is required of the artist is the cultivation of judgment, sensitivity, and an ear or an eye for the potentialities of the medium. To insist on a technical framework for art produces in students and teachers anaesthesia; the sense of aesthetic experience atrophies.

Shulman (1987) and others engaged in empirical research on teaching have identified aspects of pedagogy that resist assimilation to a technical model. Emphasizing comprehension and reasoning, transformation and reflection, Shulman argues for a complex understanding of the pedagogical act—a reasoned activity requiring a depth of knowledge that undergoes constant transformation as it becomes the object of its own reflection. He implicitly denies the legitimacy, even as a matter of conceptual convenience, of the forced disjuncture between thought and action and content and method preserved in most reform proposals.

D. Jean Clandinin's (1986) exploration of the teacher "images" that structure "personal practical knowledge" has contributed enormously to the project of developing an understanding of teaching in which reflection is held to be a central *activity* of teaching and in which theorizing takes its rightful place as a practical activity and the subject of continual dialectical transformations. Fenstermacher (1986), although maintaining a distinction between knowledge production and knowledge use, as several of his critics have noted, has provided a useful analytic scheme for describing the practical and moral dimensions of teaching. All of the research in this mode describes a complex role for the teacher—one in which teachers are responsible for decisions that actively mediate the constant conflicts among multiple, often competing, interests of students, school administrators, parents, political authorities, and others even as they strive to teach something to someone. This activity requires a kind of knowledge and attitude toward work captured in Schön's (1983) investigations of "reflective practitioners" and Sternberg's (1986) understanding of "practical intelligence." The conceptions of teaching that emerge from such work may have a great deal more to do with art than with science, or at least with science as construed in the usual objectivist fashion. They certainly have more to do with art than with a science valued chiefly for its technological applicability.

FINDING EDUCATIONAL ALTERNATIVES

If the practice of education requires a judgment, sensitivity, and familarity with the medium similar to that required in the making of art, the contemporary search for a scientific knowledge base for the preparation of teachers is misguided and will result in miseducation. Those who prepare to teach solely from such a knowledge base may become technicians or functionaries, but never professionals. In claiming something like the artist's sensibility as a developmental goal of professional education, we intend to convey the sense that professional practice consists of activities in which method and content are mutually constitutive. But we also recommend caution and the casting of a practiced critical eye over those approaches to teaching and to profession in general that take refuge in art and the fiction of the learned person—lawyer, doctor, teacher, and so forth. These approaches are as likely to produce romantic, sentimental, and educationally dangerous practitioners as the scientific approach is to produce a roster of shopkeepers and bureaucrats in our schools. They invoke a nostalgia for an American pastoral age similar to that demonstrated by the nineteenth-century reformers. They deny the knowledge that the democratization of education and the project of education for democratic participation requires that we relinquish our fantasy of the gentleman scholar and the gentleman teacher. In all such works the teacher-scholar and the student are fantastical creatures untainted by the mess and fuss of everyday life and exempt from the exigencies of survival in bureaucratic institutions. The figure of the artist in these discussions is similarly romanticized and sentimentalized. *He* is the one who stands outside of social structures and pressures—the one whose dedication is to eternal standards of truth, beauty, and morality. *He* disdains the scientist's illusion of progress through denial, only to provide an equally dangerous illusion of eternalness through psychic regression.

Many of our colleagues in liberal arts disciplines are engaged in just such a romantic, sentimental, and dangerous enterprise in their calls for a return to the verities of liberal studies, which alone can produce the habits of heart and mind that are the mark of a moral imagination. Allan Bloom's (1987) *The Closing of the American Mind* promises to have a great impact on how education is conceived and on just what liberal study is perceived to be about. Bloom means to recall us to a vision of a liberal education that can be described as none other than gentlemanly. It is a vision in which science and professional preparation sit somewhere along the margins of the frame, the center being occupied by a reconstructed humanities, reconstructed as the study of the "classics." In Bloom's proposed reconstruction, Plato's *Republic* is to be read as the educator's manual. This is not surprising, coming as it does from a person who refers to African-American student protesters at Cornell University during the 1960s as "rabble." Bloom's undemocratic approach to liberal education is precisely what must be resisted if we are to consider seriously the proposals that would in some way make liberal studies central to the project of professional preparation. Bloom, of course, understands "professional education" as a contradiction. In addition to the prestige of the natural sciences and the presence of professional studies in the university, other enemies of liberal learning are rock and roll, television, the democratization of the university, and that greatest of threats to education—feminism, the movement most subversive of "nature." That these are not the same sort of thing at all, and that their various impacts need to be assessed differently and in different contexts, will pass unnoticed by many of Bloom's readers.

Bloom's criticism of American education appeals to a nostalgic common sense and coincides with the appearance of less well known but increasingly common variations on his thought in educational literature. Many of these, in response to their understanding of the limitations of scientific approaches to education, have taken up an Aristotelian position (see Holt, 1987). That there is a *telos* in human conduct, and that it is the business of education to empower people to realize *that telos*, is compatible with Bloom's (1987) fossilized, undemocratic (and finally inaccurate) view of liberal education. All such work neglects the fact that the Aristotelian *telos* is the *telos* of *man*, and of a man who is a natural aristocrat.

Even more democratically minded critics of the narrow view of professionalization conceive of liberal study in a limited and unemancipatory fashion that takes for granted the legitimacy of Bloom's vision of a liberal curriculum, a vision with *man* as its principal subject. E. D. Hirsch's *Cultural Literacy* (1987), for example, articulates an educational project clearly understood as conservative of "culture" and "democracy." Not only are the components of "cultural literacy" those objects and understandings that define an elitist patriarchal culture; according to Hirsch, the degradation of education can be laid directly at the door of those two philosophers of democracy—Rousseau and Dewey. But a conservative view of education, we argue, is inherently undemocratic. For a democracy contains the possibility of continuous change and enlargement of "culture." A democracy contains the potential for its own positive transformation; a democratic education, whether liberal or professional, enables persons to act on that potential.

Hirsch argues that his vision is not exclusive. He claims that we have a moral obligation to be certain that all members of our society are in possession of negotiable common currency. We use this language of economics deliberately. One must be bemused when Hirsch—in noting proudly that his father, a businessman, was able to quote Shakespeare regularly in his business communications—can find no better justification for his inclination to do so than that Shakespeare is more persuasive in his writing than most American businessmen. As does Bloom, Hirsch and others uncritically accept patriarchal culture as culture; thus his claim of inclusion is an inclusion that would assimilate all to a particular set of experiences. But such inclusion, as any number of women and other minorities have argued, requires of students a denial of their own real lives and experiences. There is an inversion at work here in which the price of inclusion is exclusion. As liberal studies are conceived by such writers as Bloom and Hirsch, they are conceived as conserving and transmitting the most valuable of our cultural traditions—and usually as an end in themselves, as having a *telos* contained within and achieved through their very forms and content. It is assumed that the subjects constituting liberal inquiry deal with general—that is, universal—human questions about the nature of human beings, right conduct, life in accord with nature. These studies are often treated as if the questions raised by them are, just as are scientific questions, context-free. That is, liberal inquiry is presumed to be unaffected by particular social, historical, and political exigencies, the "human condition" with all of its dilemmas and prospects being read as simultaneously subtending and transcending local concerns.

Studies in the traditional liberal arts disciplines are seen to involve general, enduring, and critical human questions about which we may seek guidance from philosophers, historians, theologians, and other eminent scholars. Such studies are regarded as intrinsically valuable, to be pursued for the excellence of mind, beauty of soul, and pleasure to the learner they will afford. These are self-validating studies. Through study in the liberal disciplines, through conversation with "the best that has been thought and said" (Arnold, 1869/1932), the student will become open-minded—not in the sense of being meekly tolerant or indifferent, but in being passionately committed to honest inquiry dedicated to making the world a better place; not because he (our educated gentleman) knows how to *do* anything in particular, but simply because he has *become* a certain sort of person. Through liberal study, the cultural heritage and the ethos of a nation are inscribed in the minds and the hearts of students so as to ensure right conduct. More recently, liberal inquiry has been regarded as essential to comprehension of the rhetorics and methods of the various disciplines and of the history of the methodology of the pursuit of knowledge itself.

We should note an interesting and not incidental inconsistency. One is not to ask what one can do with a major in philosophy, literature and so forth. These studies are not to *do* with, but to *be*. At the same time, there is that sense that education ought to prepare one *for* something. In American culture, to be and to do are such worlds apart that we find it not inconsistent to say of someone that he is a good man who has committed the following heinous acts. The wisdom of psychologists tells us that it will never do to say that someone is bad but only that he does bad things. A liberal education prepares us to be, and that will be the foundation of our doing.

LIBERAL AND PROFESSIONAL STUDIES

Contrary to such views, we argue that a liberal education is, or should be, practical, preparing the student for active participation in the making of the world—for doing and being at the same time. Fundamental to this project is the development of a moral imagination, in teachers as well as in students. Persons who act out of a moral imagination (and we shall argue that a moral imagination is essential to professional practice) act in accord with practical reason. In this, we are urging a reconceptualized view of liberal education as well as of professional practice. In our view, the practice of teaching should be taken as a central object of liberal study and liberal study should be taken as the object of teaching. "Profession" describes at once a knowing and a doing; it describes a practice rather than a technical application. The sense of "profession" as we encounter it in the literature of professionalization is a debased one. There the professions seem to be narrowly concerned with the inculcation of habits and the development of skills from which competent practice within a vocation will result. While those concerned with the study and the teaching of the liberal arts tend to see themselves as engaged actively in the life of the mind, in developing in students certain desirable habits of mind and heart, those concerned with professional training are often inclined to see themselves as simply certifying some sort of technical competence among graduates who have been taught to accomplish specific vocational tasks through the deployment of acquired skills. Such a notion of "vocation," too, is debased. For one should not ignore the etymological, therefore epistemological and ethical, relationship of both words to the sense of calling.

According to the *Oxford English Dictionary*, the earliest uses of *profess* have to do with entering a religious order and with proclaiming vows. After 1500, it becomes possible to use the word in the context of any public declaration or avowal. Many of these uses have to do with professions of attachment or friendship. After 1500, also, one who claims a profession makes a claim to knowledge, and that claim is intimately related to one's communal attachments. A profession is "a vocation in which a professed knowledge of some department of learning or science is used in its application to the affairs of others or in the practice of an art founded upon it." The neglect of these senses of *profess* has been detrimental to professional life. It was not until the nineteenth century that *profession* was isolated from its communal attachments and from a notion of "general cultivation." *Profession* then came to be used humorously or derogatorily, as in the "profession of muffin baking."

The nineteenth century was a time during which preparations for many occupations formerly considered trades, notably elementary teaching, were admitted as subjects of university education and accorded professional status, however lowly such status may have been. The twentieth century has seen a proliferation of such professions. The history of professionalization cannot be understood apart from the history of industrialization, a history marked by increasing segmentation of social and economic function, a history in which the contemplative life and the life of action finally diverged completely, a history in which the divergence of knowing and acting became naturalized. The division of labor, which emerged with the collectivization of labor in the factory, came to pervade all areas of social existence and all social practices.

Our present-day notions of profession are inextricably bound to the division of labor. The historical processes through which professional labor emerged and congealed have been documented by Lasch (1984), Edwards (1979), and Noble (1984), among others. These studies point to the questions of trust raised in professional relationships and to the way in which "professionalization" attempts to create in technical expertise a substitute for the necessity for trust even as it renders helpless the professional's clients. An increasingly complex and fragmented social world is described, one in which the public and private are wrenched apart and persons are left alone with themselves and unsure of what to do with their privacy. As personal life becomes increasingly privatized, the common lore that sustains a community is no longer available. Increasingly the business of sustaining and building community is given over to (or co-opted by) those presumed to have a special expertise. If one wants to plant a garden, raise one's children, undertake a program of exercise and diet, or save one's marriage, one enrolls in a class or pays a fee to the expert presumed to know. Lasch (1984) refers to this phenomenon as "socialized incompetence." If all are incompetent except experts, then one has no choice but to pay the fee. And trust comes to be based on technical expertise rather than bonds of community and caring.

But as recent history in the professions demonstrates, technical expertise is a poor substitute for the bonds of community on which alone trust can be based. This is an educational matter. We have only to look at the problems of law and medicine (the professions on which much of the reform proposals have been modeled) to understand the limitations of a purely technical approach and its failure to substitute for the bonds of trust and care that must characterize any professional relationship. It is the business of education to consolidate and make explicit those bonds and the moral obligations they carry. Surgeons may be wonderfully adept with their tools, but they cannot engender patients' trust without an understanding of the human situation in which the patients find themselves. For this reason any number of medical and law schools are requiring courses that compel future practitioners to study questions traditionally assigned to the humanities. Even the Harvard Business School now offers a course taught by Jerome Bruner in which students read novels, such as *Babbitt*, that explore the social and psychic costs of their professional ethos and practice.

A central commitment of ours is to honor and help achieve the spirit of profession. At the same time, liberal inquiry must lead students into the world; indeed, it must produce in them the habits of heart and mind conducive to humane and responsible participation in democratic structures. Professional studies must, then, contain a liberal agenda and aim, and liberal studies must prepare students to profess—in all modes of their participation in life. Because both professional and liberal education are at present too narrowly conceived, the liberating and humanistic aims of the liberal arts are subverted, while professional education has lost sight of the human spirit which is, or ought to be, the object of all education. As we proceed through our various analyses and arguments, one of the things we shall consider is the way in which educational institutions and practices themselves sustain

the separate-spheres approach to professional and liberal education—an approach harmful to teachers in both spheres. This
consideration will involve an excavation of the political, social,
economic, and conceptual assumptions that are hidden under the
civilization of separate spheres. Having uncovered and deci-
phered the shards of thought and commitment beneath this civilization, we will then reformulate our understanding of both
professional and liberal education—a reformulation whereby we
hope to begin to both build a new professional culture and enlarge the notion of liberal study.

We will not be concerned with abstract, presumably universal knowledge, but with human understanding within specific
contexts and with the understanding of the practical consequences of the *act of understanding*. Human understanding and the
understanding of its practical consequences, we argue, is fundamental to professional study. This is not simply an expression of
preference. We are convinced that the picture of knowledge, both
in the professions and in liberal studies—where knowledge is
represented as universal, objective, and transcending context—is
neither credible nor politically and morally defensible. Much critical work recently—and this volume comes out of that critical
tradition—has explored the ways in which observation and judgments regarding observations change as we challenge the canons
of our disciplines. The inclusion of women and workers and
people of color in history has changed not only what we know
about history (the content); it has also changed the ways in which
historians do history (the methods). The range of questions considered "philosophically interesting" has been considerably en-
larged by a body of feminist philosophy that challenges the Pla-
tonic vision of the metropolis of the mind in which right reason
justly rules over all. The assaults on the canon by feminist and
poststructural literary theorists have forever changed the teaching of literature. Even biology looks very different from the way
it did 20 years ago, and not because of incremental accretions to
knowledge and technology (see, for example, Bernstein, 1983;
Bleier, 1984; Greene, 1981; Harding, 1986; Keller, 1983, 1985;
Rorty, 1979). When we know that liberal studies cannot be
understood apart from structures of gender, class, and racial
relations, we connect liberal study truly to the possibilities of
emancipation and transformation promised in our college catalogues. At the same time, those who practice the profession of
teaching must have learned to study, to read, to know, and to act

in ways that express such an understanding of the contingent nature of knowledge. The ways that we conceive of knowledge, the ways that we formulate our questions, are unavoidably affected by the social, political, and economic frameworks within which we come to know and to know ourselves as knower-actors.

If we deny the importance of such contexts, we do not escape their influence. Instead, the prejudices that sustain those contexts contaminate both discourse and action without our recognizing the symptoms of contamination. We learn to live with our poisons. For example, in claiming the "best that has been thought and said" as the content of the liberal arts, we fail to acknowledge the inclusionary and exclusionary choices that resulted in those "best" judgments. In relegating professional study to the acquisition of technical skills, we neglect the social and moral dimensions of professional practice; we avoid fundamental questions of trust and care in the professional relationship. For these reasons, a technicized view of profession and a rarefied view of liberal study offer little hope of a responsive, progressive engagement with current inadequacies.

Teaching is essentially social, moral, and political. The transmission of the cultural heritage, even the transmission of professional lore and standards, involves the formation of character, the initiation of persons into ways of constructing the worlds in which they and others will live. Teaching involves more than the transmission of skills. Skills, information, texts, activities—the purpose of all of those things must be seen as enabling students to become choosers in a world in which their choices must matter. We hope that they will learn to make good choices—as teachers, as parents, as friends, as lovers. But this is a judgment that no technical skill will help us with. We are saying that it is the business of education to enable persons to develop and exercise practical reason. Such a business demands the exercise of practical reason by its practitioners.

AN OVERVIEW OF THIS BOOK

Each of the following chapters in this volume proceeds from the assumption that the aim of all education is the development of practical reason. In professional education, the aim is something we will call practical competence, a competence that can be defined generally for all professions even as we account for the specific demands of individual professions. In our account of practical competence, we necessarily invoke those attributes typically reserved for liberal studies. We are talking about developing modes of reasoning in which thought and action, content and method, theory and practice stand in a dialogical relationship to one another, a mode of reasoning in which liberal study is itself a variety of profession. We argue that in teaching, as in other professional endeavors, the necessary *practical* competence demands much more from liberal education than the vague cultivation of humane and well-rounded individuals. Although Sternberg (1986), Schön (1983), and others have begun referring to "practical intelligence" and dimensions of "artistry," they nonetheless continue to refer to judgments of *technique*, however tacit or variable. Drawing from theoretical traditions informed by hermeneutics, we can identify a distinct competence ("phronesis") for *practical* (as opposed to technical or instrumental) judgment and action. For the competent practitioner previous understandings of general principles, social and personal interests, and valued *ends* themselves are always open to dialogical reinterpretation in their *hermeneutical* application to the contingent circumstances in which ends, interests, or principles are implemented and pursued (as opposed to *technical* application, or the "application" of techniques for attaining prespecified ends). Donald Schön (1983) does provide examples that illustrate such differences between technical and practical rationality, but his language of "artistry" fails to specify the kind of dialogical competence required for interpersonal and social praxis. Instead of using technical means to accomplish prespecified ends, professionals must have the competence to assist in the praxis of progressive reinterpretation of their clients' projects and interests. Praxis refers to the conduct of social life, with all of its political and ethical dimensions. It refers to a mode of knowing in which knowing is a form of social conduct, in which it is an enactment of social relations.[1]

---

[1]According to the *Random House Dictionary of the English Language* (Second Edition, Unabridged, 1987), *praxis* means "act" or "action" in Greek and medieval Latin, but the English definition is "1. practice, as distinguished from theory; application or use, as of knowledge or skills. 2. convention, habit, or custom." Usage that more adequately reflects the real existential referents of *praxis* requires working against some deeply embedded habits and conventions of the English language itself, as we (and, regrettably, our readers) must labor to do here. Fortunately, the *Random House Dictionary* does offer a more adequate definition of *phronesis*, as "wisdom in determining ends and the means of attaining them."

The chapters that comprise this book are not to be read as individual productions embodying distinct and separable themes. This book is not an expression of individual voices, but rather the result of conversation and elaboration through which variations on a central theme are woven together.

In the next chapter we elucidate a model for the study of education as a liberal discipline. We develop a picture of educational studies against a social landscape in which what we know is implicated in what we do (Feinberg, 1983). As a liberal study, the study of education brings us to an awareness of the dialogical relationships between theory and practice, content and method, and being and doing and urges us to a critical perspective. This representation of educational study is situated in a scene of interpretation in which what we know must always be known with an attitude of epistemological humility, which alone expresses a commitment to democratic social arrangements. In this view, the study of education itself becomes a kind of praxis and the model of liberal study.

In Chapter 3, we explore the functionalist and empiricist foundations for mainstream views of the professions. In a comparative analysis of such occupations as law and medicine, we argue that the authority and autonomy aimed for in professionalization do not accrue to persons and occupations on the basis of advanced, specialized, and technical knowledge. This argument proceeds from a recognition that while practical competence requires professional autonomy and authority, technical proficiency does not. Such an analysis leads to a view of professionalism recognized as the social praxis of those who are relied on for a dialogical interpretation of multiple, competing interests.

As professionals, then, teachers must learn to mediate their students' relationship to the curriculum and its content as well as their participation in the social order of the school. The teacher's preparation, consequently, must include competent praxis as a student of the liberal arts, as the latter are depicted in Chapter 2. These issues are taken up in Chapter 4.

In Chapter 5, our formulation of education as a liberal study is employed to argue that liberal study must acknowledge the specific relationships of particular students to language, to learning, and to the pedagogical relationships out of which language and learning are produced. This is a feminist analysis, one that reformulates the rhetoric of liberal education by exposing the interested nature of the binary oppositions in which the rhetoric is cast so as to displace them. In deconstructing this rhetoric, we expose its contradictory, exclusionary, and assimilative tendencies and illustrate the structural similarities of this view to our understanding of the profession of teaching. In so doing we make problematic the very act of teaching, particularly for those who are excluded from the content they must teach. We conclude by addressing the question of trust as it relates to the practical competence discussed in Chapters 3 and 4. Here we articulate an understanding of practical reason that defies the patriarchal assumptions inherent in the Aristotelian notion.

In the final chapter we present a critical analysis of the historical tension between professionalized preparation for teachers and liberal education. In addition, we present new models of teacher education that have as their object the reconstruction of practical reason. In these projects professional courses become foundational, not in the sense of determining truth or reason, but in the sense of developing a theory of practice and a practice of theory. Teaching is here understood as a "field of action" related to what is referred to as a "narrative field." Within these "fields" content and method are united. Both theoretical and practical work are treated as modes of being, knowing, and acting that yield a genuinely reflective practice. To know is to profess and to profess is to know, and to profess and to know are to be responsible for the worlds we construct. This is a view that acknowledges the normative nature of both teaching and teacher preparation and that opposes teacher education to teacher training.

A major point of this volume is that the liberal education of teachers, as liberal education is defined in this volume, is essential. A related point is that a similar liberal education is necessary for all concerned with the education of the young—teachers, parents, university professors, politicians, journalists, and even educational researchers. It is our wish to end the bifurcations that characterize present discourse and to acknowledge and accept responsibility for the practical consequences of our knowledge.

CHAPTER 2

Education as a Liberal Field of Study

There is a view, common among academics and educators alike, that education is but an applied area of study, one in which the methods of the traditional disciplines are used to address school-related problems. Education is seen as such because it is said to have no methodological principles or conceptual domain that it can call its own. Unlike such fields as physics or chemistry or economics, which are thought of as pure disciplines with applied wings, education is thought to be unbounded. It cannot claim to be examining bodily motion, or the interaction of elements, or market behavior. Similarly, it is argued that education as a field is deficient because it can lay no claim to a unique methodology. Experimental design, statistical methods, or ethnographic techniques do not belong first to education. They are methods developed in other areas that are sometimes useful in addressing issues and problems that we find in schools. Because educational studies are said to lack both a conceptual domain and an identifiable method, they are thought to have no coherent research program. Rather, they must take their problems from the schools as the schools provide them. Thus it is concluded that with education we have a "discipline" without a method, without substance, and without coherence.

We state this position so strongly not simply because we want to take issue with it and argue that the study of education, while applicable to the practices of schools, is consistent with the notion of a liberal field of study, but also because this is a view of education found in many of our most important academic institutions. Too often education exists on the periphery of academic life, perceived as a field comprising renegades from the schools and outcasts from the disciplines.

To take exception to this view is to begin to define a direction for the study of education, a direction that one can already find in the ongoing work of many educational scholars but that requires articulation and development. In this chapter we want to address the question of the place of educational studies within a college or university. We begin by looking at the question of the relationship between a discipline and its method and domain. We then address the question of the domain of educational studies as we have been trying to conceptualize it and sketch some of its major features. Finally, we draw out some of the implications of this domain for the practical aspects of education.

ACADEMIC DISCIPLINES AND METHODOLOGIES

It is useful to note that the ideal of a discipline against which educational studies has been measured and found wanting is, in fact, an ideal that accepted disciplines meet only to varying degrees. In some disciplines, such as philosophy, the nature of the conceptual domain is often a central issue of debate. Ironically, without a prior understanding of the boundaries of the discipline, it is difficult to decide just who can and who cannot legitimately participate in that debate.

Other disciplines, such as economics, have been able to stipulate a realm that meets with broad consensus among its practitioners. Yet the borders of a conceptual realm, even when well defined, may not always map well onto the activities of practical life, and disciplinary neatness may be accomplished at a considerable cost. Consider, for example, the ups and downs of a plan proposed by economist Alan Enthoven (1980) to hold down the rate of increase of hospital costs. Enthoven's plan seemed to fit well into the view of rational, market behavior adopted by the Reagan administration, and it met with acclaim from key officials of that administration. Yet as the plan was discussed within the administration, some elements of it, such as a ceiling on the tax write-offs businesses could claim for health insurance, were seriously questioned and likely to be dropped. Enthoven (1982) saw this behavior as irrational. His plan was not meant to be implemented piecemeal; its effectiveness depended, according to him, on viewing each of its elements as part of a coherent whole. Yet one suspects that from the administration's point of view what was occurring was not irrational. Rather, the boundaries of economic rationality had spilled over into the field of political rationality.

Do we pass such problems over to the political scientist to understand, as if we were passing a baton from one runner to the next in a relay race? If so, we still have to decide whether politically rational behavior consists of generating the broadest support for the plan as Enthoven conceived it or of retaining only those elements of the plan for which support is likely. The answer to this question will depend on the conception of rationality that particular political scientists bring to bear on the issue.

Some social scientists have tried to argue that there is a single, broadly based concept of rational behavior (Homans, 1982). For example, some have argued that the behavior of groups, be it economic, social, or political behavior, can be reduced to the behavior of individuals as governed by the laws of positive and negative reinforcement. This conception of rationality may be useful for redescribing events, but as a conception of rational behavior it is wanting. This is because what constitutes positive or negative reinforcement is not the foundation of an explanation—that is, an invariable law of human nature. It is, rather, the product of a human interpretation. In one culture pork is an important source of nutrition. In another, to eat it is sacrilegious. Human beings have a remarkable capacity to turn what behaviorists identify as positive reinforcers into negative ones and negative reinforcers into positive ones, and this in turn is what often needs to be understood.

It is useful when thinking about the nature of a discipline to remember that the boundaries of disciplinary rationality do not always correspond to those of practical rationality and that when the latter overstep the limits of the former our understanding is not always improved by passing the problem to the next discipline. This observation does not provide educational studies with an advantage over other areas. It simply raises questions about its presumed disadvantage.

If the relationship between a discipline and a domain is problematic, then so too is the relationship between a discipline and a method. For example, not so long ago some renegade economists claimed that if we really want to know about market behavior we should try to understand, through observational studies, just how people think and behave when they act in the marketplace; a rather novel approach for "the dismal science." One can imagine the next generation of economists trading in their computers for the newest technological innovation—a credible informant—and tramping off to an Indonesian village with Clifford Geertz to learn the techniques of participant-observation. The example may be far-fetched, but the point is not: There is at best a loose connection between a discipline and a method. Historians use statistics, anthropologists use history, and often by so doing their own disciplines are enriched.

The difficulty is not that *real* disciplines have a clear-cut domain and education does not. Nor does each discipline, except education, have a single, clear and identifiable method. Domains are not sealed in cement and distributed one to a discipline. They are convenient ways that have been developed for marking off and thinking about the natural and the cultural worlds. They are no doubt bounded in some ways, but the boundaries are best thought of as open in texture, allowing for nourishment, growth, and division to take place. Similarly, a method is a tool. Its function is to serve a particular purpose, but its use and refinement may extend well beyond the purpose for which it was originally developed. A method may originate because of the problems that arise in a given discipline at a certain time, but it does not emerge with a deed of ownership that it presents to its developer. One discipline does not borrow the methods of another, because, without a title of ownership, no discipline can stand in the position of lender.

THE DOMAIN OF EDUCATIONAL STUDIES

The difficulty of establishing educational studies as a liberal field comes not from want of method or lack of domain, but from equally important, yet sometimes conflicting expectations. The first of these is the scholarship required to add perspective to and improve our understanding of the processes and aims of education as it functions in social life. The second has to do with the social responsibility to maintain and improve the schools. While these tasks are related, they are not the same. We should expect that some of the scholarly perspective will be drawn from a better understanding of the practice of schooling, just as we should also expect that a deeper understanding of the activity and aims of education will help to refine that practice. Yet to understand education requires more than an analysis of what happens in schools, and sometimes what is of immediate practical value for schooling does not require a great deal of scholarly sophistication. In theory this expectation is not different from that which we have about legal scholarship. We expect that the thoughtful study of the law will inform the judicial system and help provide some of the insights needed to improve it. Yet legal scholarship extends well beyond the law as it functions in the courts of one's own time or location. In doing so it provides a context for understanding the present legal system. The difference between educational and legal scholarship lies in the fact that educational work has too often been judged by its promise for immediate payoffs. It is more appropriate, however, to acknowledge that the activities of the schools are but one of the practices that such scholarship seeks to understand and that as part of an organized, compulsory system of education, schools are relatively recent educational innovations.

When one attempts to articulate a domain for educational studies it is useful to observe that academic domains are constituted in different ways. Some domains, especially those of the natural sciences, focus on a single attribute or characteristic of an object. Here we are interested in an object only insofar as it is a manifestation of that characteristic. In classical physics, for example, the actual object is irrelevant (it may be an apple, a rock, or a planet) except, say, insofar as it is a manifestation of bodily motion. Other domains are constituted as an attempt to understand an object in its fullness and uniqueness and to capture the contours of significance that the object itself holds. These disciplines comprise what are often called the cultural sciences. Each of these ways of constituting a discipline carries with it methodological implications, and the problems of confusing one with the other are well illustrated by Clifford Geertz (1973), drawing on an example developed by Gilbert Ryle.

> Consider . . . two boys rapidly contracting the eyelids of the right eye. In one this is an involuntary twitch; in the other, a conspiratorial signal to a friend. The two movements are, as movements, identical; from an I-am-a-Camera, "phenomenalistic" observation of them alone, one could not tell which was twitch and which was wink. Yet the difference, however un-

photographable, between a twitch and a wink is vast; as everyone unfortunate enough to have had the first taken for the
second knows. The winker is communicating and indeed communicating in a quite precise and special way. . . . The winker
has not done two things, contracted his eyelids and winked,
while the twitcher has done only one, contracted his eyelids.
Contracting your eyelids on purpose when there exists a public
code in which doing so counts as a conspiratorial signal *is*
winking. (p. 6)

Educational scholarship has tended to vacillate between these
views. Sometimes the emphasis is placed on methods that are
thought to have significant power to generalize and predict,
while at other times the emphasis has been to capture the unique
contours of a particular learning situation. For the most part,
however, in both types of study the school and its activities have
been taken as defining the domain of educational research, and
each study has difficulty transcending the school's definition of
an educational problem.

A more fruitful way to constitute the domain of educational
studies is to attempt, through the identification of a common
function, to capture the universal features that are represented
by the practice of education while also recognizing the various
forms that these features may take in specific situations. After
all, even the most committed ethnographers must presuppose
some shared, intercultural categories as they go about trying to
understand the uniqueness of social life. In other words, there
must be some taken-for-granted categories that allow us to describe even the most unique social units and to classify certain
people as members of that society rather than simply as an
aggregate of individuals. For example, to recognize that a certain
ceremony is to be taken humorously or ironically, rather than
seriously or literally, is to place it in a general category that
transcends the specific and unique culture in which it is being
performed.

It is the attempt to identify the universal aspects of educational practice that constitutes the important feature of those
studies that look upon education as the process of socialization or
cultural transmission. However, these studies represent only a
partial understanding of educational practice and are mistaken in
viewing the study of education itself as simply a part of sociology
or anthropology.

Studies of socialization and of cultural transmission have tended to focus on the ways in which an individual becomes a member of a group. Accepting the structure of social relations as fixed and unproblematic, they concentrate on analyzing just how an individual takes on the behavior and roles that society defines as appropriate. Whereas the society is perceived as fixed and unchanging, the individual is seen as adaptable to any structure that can develop a sufficient socializing apparatus.

What is missing from this account is the fact that society itself is continually re-created, although not always in the same form, through a shared understanding in which all of its members, to one degree or another, and within different frameworks, participate. The production of a society is a function of the development of such shared understanding, and this production is the primary function of education, first as a social activity and only later as a social institution. Thus, while it is productive to view educational studies in terms of an analysis of a universal feature of social life, individual socialization is only a derivative aspect of that study. That is, educational studies is conceived of here as the study of the ways in which a society reproduces itself over time and of the various patterns of understanding that compose the product of that reproduction.

In order to understand what this entails we can return briefly to look at the notion of socialization and distinguish it from that of social reproduction. One distinction is obvious. Individuals are socialized, but a society is reproduced. When we are studying social reproduction, we are examining the normative structure into which individuals are socialized. If we look again at the process of socialization, we should begin to see where it intersects with that of social reproduction.

To be socialized is to learn a role or set of roles, along with the behavior appropriate to it. Yet socialization also involves learning how one's own role functions in relationship to others and learning that in any specific situation appropriate role behavior is defined relationally. A simple example is that behavior appropriate for a corporal in the presence of a private is not always appropriate in the presence of a captain. This means that a key factor in learning the set of behaviors that define a given role is learning when it is appropriate to exhibit a specific subset of that behavior. What this suggests, however, is that when socialization occurs what is learned is not just a set of behaviors, but a set of socially shared categories and definitions that are understood relationally to one another, such as worker to owner, husband to wife, mother to daughter, and so forth. What remains to be understood after the sociologists have done their work are the patterns of understanding out of which role behavior is generated. These patterns and the processes used to reproduce them constitute the domain of educational studies.

The study of education as social reproduction is the study of patterns and processes through which a society's identity is maintained and within which social change is defined. The practice of education in this sense has two functions. First, there is the reproduction of skills that meet socially defined needs. Second, there is the reproduction of consciousness, or the shared understanding that provides the basis of social life. This shared understanding includes the sense that people have of the interrelationship and purpose of different skills, of their different social positions, and of the form proper behavior takes in different contexts (Feinberg, 1983). The task of educational scholarship, however, is not restricted simply to reflecting such forms or understanding them in precisely the same way as those who participate in them fully. In contrast to the unreflective and naturalistic understanding of the participant, the function of educational scholarship is to understand these relationships as social constructions with historical antecedents and thereby to initiate an awareness that these patterns, or at least some of them, are objects of choice and possible candidates for change. Thus educational scholarship adds a reflectively critical dimension to the social activity of education.

A comprehensive analysis of education for any given society would include an examination of the structure, production, and distribution of knowledge as well as the scope of knowledgeable activity and the level of knowledge that is presumed to attach to given social roles. Thus the study of education as social reproduction examines both the way in which knowledge is produced and the way in which it is distributed in a society. For example, physicians and nurses are presumed to share knowledge over essentially the same range of activity, that is, the scope of their knowledge is similar. However, their knowledge about the disease process and its treatment is thought to be at different levels, a difference that is reflected in the formal education and status of the two groups. Whereas the concept of scope describes the nature of the field over which knowledge is exercised, the concept of level differentiates the roles within a field and provides an understanding of the variations in status that are attached to different roles. Hence, using health care again as an example, while one of the major functions of physicians is to prescribe medication, they are usually not prohibited from dispensing it, at least in small doses; the institutional assumption is that the knowledge involved in dispensing is available to physicians. The pharmacist, however, is restricted to dispensing on order from the physician; the institutional assumption is that the act of prescribing is beyond his or her trained capacity.

One can often understand the conflicts between established and aspiring professions as involving attempts to alter perceptions about the scope or level of knowledge possessed by a given group. Such conflicts often involve a challenge to the institutionally sanctioned presumptions about knowledge. Hence, in arguing the case for greater professional autonomy, nurses deny that physicians and nurses share the same scope of knowledge. Physicians are said to be proficient in clinical judgments related to crisis intervention, while nurses are seen as experts in the social and cultural factors that affect the way in which patients cope with disease. Similarly, pharmacists attempt to affirm their independence over physicians by claiming a greater level of understanding about the interactions of drugs. Such challenges are really attempts to rearrange the skills associated with a given role and hence to change the way in which the role is perceived.

The educational system, both formal and informal, reproduces and distributes (or redistributes) skills as they are clustered into roles; thus it maintains or alters the work relations in society. Included within the reproduction of skills is the reproduction of ideas about the ownership of knowledge and about the rights and responsibilities of those who possess certain forms of institutionally granted knowledge. This aspect of education may be seen as the reproduction of consciousness.

Thus the reproduction of consciousness is the other side of the reproduction of skills. It is the factor that enables the clustering of skills into specific roles and the clustering of roles into specific classes to persist in societies by providing the normative vision that justifies the existing distribution. In other words, a consciousness is reproduced that codes the exercise of the rights, privileges, duties, and obligations associated with the possession of a certain set of skills as just, fair, and acceptable (or, in unstable societies, as unjust, unfair, and unacceptable). The term "knowledge code" is intended to suggest that education imparts, in addition to a set of skills, a certain mode of consciousness, a way of thinking, about the network of such skills. We learn, for example, what is high- and low-status knowledge; we also learn, either through manner, mode of expression, dress, or physical environment, how to appraise and communicate with people with differently valued skills. We learn the range of activity over which a person with a certain level of knowledge is to be granted authority. Thus a knowledge code ideally binds together the reproduction of skills and the reproduction of consciousness, and its formal articulation is to be understood as an interrelated body of arguments and beliefs about the relative value and interrelationship of different skills. Formal education can be understood as a consciously designed and institutionalized system of instruction that functions to maintain a given knowledge code and to further the pattern of intellectual development that is associated with it.

IMPLICATIONS FOR EDUCATIONAL PRACTICE

With this basic sketch behind us, we now turn to look at some of the different kinds of projects that may be suggested by it. The struggle between the medical and nursing professions, mentioned earlier, is a useful place to begin. The attempt by nurses to achieve greater independence from doctors can be understood in part as an effort to redefine the knowledge code involved in health care delivery by disengaging the knowledge base of nursing from that of medicine, reclustering the skills associated with the role of the nurse, and reworking the professional consciousness of nurses and physicians.

The difficulty that nurses have had in establishing their own professional identity can be understood largely in terms of the institutional assumption that nursing knowledge is simply a subset of medical knowledge, an assumption now being challenged by many nurses. The developments now occurring provide an opportunity for educational scholars to analyze the process whereby a group sets out consciously to redefine its essential knowledge base. The issues that this attempt involves are many. There are questions about the reworking of basic definitions of health and disease; there are issues about the relative worth of clinical, scientific, and social science knowledge in health care; there is the question of the way in which professional dominance and male dominance intermingle in the relations between occupational groups; and there are questions about the implications that an emerging professional identity has for formal educational structures.

One way to think more generally about the issues developing in health care is to recognize that different groups and individuals, depending on the nature of their developed skills, stand in different relations to a knowledge code and view it through different frames. Because of this, a knowledge code has built into it a potential instability. Most segments of society will be expected to take on faith the fact that the definition and distribution of high-status knowledge is justified; but with the exception of the initiated, most will only be able to view such knowledge from the outside. As long as there is a general acceptance that the clustering of skills and the definition and distribution of high-status knowledge compose a natural process or are of functional benefit to all, stability will likely remain. As in the case of the many nurses who still identify closely with the medical profession, this stability is an indication of a tight bond between a code and its relevant frames.

Yet because a frame provides a perspective for viewing a knowledge code, it is always possible that the dominant code or some aspect of it will be denaturalized and seen as just another framework, one that belongs to and simply rationalizes the position of the dominant social group. It is interesting that some medical students whom one of the authors has interviewed see the basic medical science courses in this way, as simply an initiation rite without functional value. Were this perception to be held on a large scale it would signal a crisis of confidence within the profession, and the potential instability of a knowledge code might begin to erupt from within as it became disengaged from those who are expected to be its prime bearers.

The instability of a code is not, however, simply a function of the way in which it is tied to its relevant frames. It is also a function of the way in which those who are antagonistic to a dominant code are able to communicate their individual frameworks to one another. Such communication is often the major weapon of informal cultural groups, occurring both in the classroom and the workplace, and it often takes the sophisticated skills of an ethnographer to decipher it. When there is good reason to believe that there is not a radical difference between the official meanings of the dominant code and the shared meanings of the relevant frames, then it seems appropriate to apply standardized research procedures. However, when such congruence cannot be assumed, it is difficult for standard procedures to capture the event. For example, the efficiency engineer can describe in detail the formal, task-directed behaviors of the workers on the shop-floor; and when the workers share the basic goals of the enterprise, this may be all that is required. When such goals are not shared, however, what the efficiency engineer cannot capture are the swaggers and posturing his or her very presence triggers. Indeed, if they are timed correctly, the engineer will simply take these swaggers as the natural behavior of working-class people. Yet it is precisely this posturing that serves as the network through which these people may communicate to one another their shared framework of antagonism. The presence of the engineer is, of course, for them simply the symbol of the object of this antagonism, that is, the basic goals and purposes of the organization. The other side of this process involves the design of formal bureaucratic organizations, which are often structured in such a way as to minimize the possibility of lateral communication.

By identifying the domain of educational studies as that of social reproduction, it is possible to focus the concerns of educational scholarship and to cement its interdisciplinary character. The study of education as social reproduction shifts the basic unity of these disciplines from a strictly pragmatic one, which is called into operation to repair dysfunctions in the schools, to an organic one, in which each discipline focuses on a different moment in the reproductive process. The problems of schools are not forgotten, however, because in contemporary society they compose a major vehicle for social reproduction.

Using such a conception, educational philosophy might be concerned with analyzing the formal coherence of the knowledge code, while also exploring some of the conceptual ambiguities and problems that might be concealed by it. Educational history could attempt to explore the forces that were instrumental in its development, while studies in literature could explore the way in which, through metaphor and other communicative structures, a code is extended from one area of study to another. The social sciences might be concerned with understanding the way in which the present code extends or limits possibilities for different segments of the social order, while the behavioral sciences might attempt to elaborate the way in which present forms of reproduction and the present distribution of skills influence the frames through which the existing code is perceived.

The important point, however, is not the particular way in which the various disciplinary traditions might decide to distribute the conceptual domain of education. It is, rather, that the work of these disciplines and their problematics are altered by recognizing the existence of a reasonably clear domain for educational studies. A clearer understanding of the domain provides educational studies with a more coherent program, regardless of the particular discipline or method needed at a given time.

Moreover, an understanding of the variety of frameworks that children bring with them to school has some important implications for understanding classroom behavior and for helping to improve the teaching process. For example, different frameworks will often entail different rules about the context in which truth-telling is appropriate, and even what constitutes telling the truth. Where there is a presumption of shared antagonism and illegitimate authority, saying what happened will be seen not as telling the truth but as acknowledging submissiveness. Whether saying what happened will be taken as truth-telling will depend on who says it, in what setting, and to whom it is said. This is the case in the classroom, the shop, and the corporation. For example, in the corporation certain matters may be widely, but privately, acknowledged to be the case. However, to utter these matters publicly would be viewed not as truth-telling but as indiscretions or signs of untrustworthiness. The reason for this is not too difficult to analyze formally. There are important practical differences between (1) my knowing something is the case; (2) my knowing that you also know it is the case; (3) my knowing that you know that I know it is the case; and (4) your and my knowing that it is publicly known that together we know it is the case. Each of these stages comes closer to forcing choice and action. If teachers understand these formal aspects, they will not be prone to label as deviant children with a somewhat different set of truth-telling rules. In other words, teachers need to know what may be at stake in certain instances where truth-telling and displays of other values are being called for.

That the understanding of classroom behavior can often be improved by understanding the interaction between an official code and its relevant frames can be illustrated through Paul Willis's (1981) study of working-class boys in an English school. The focus of Willis's ethnographic account was a small subgroup of troublemakers who called themselves "the lads." When order was maintained in this school, as is the case with most, it was because the students' own cultural framework allowed them to accept the basic knowledge code as articulated by teachers. The official, but sometimes implicit, message of the school was that if students respected the teacher's authority, the teacher would provide them with worthwhile (usually theoretical) knowledge that would lead to a meaningful credential, which would then lead to a promising job. For the lads, however, this exchange broke down. For them one job was the same as any other (as one of them put it after a lecture on becoming an interior decorator, "got to be someone who slops on walls"); hence the credential was meaningless, the knowledge literally useless, and the respect bogus. For most students in the school, order, discipline, and truth-telling as teachers defined them were part of the bargain. The lads, however, viewed them as complicity with an illegitimate authority and a violation of their own group norms.

Willis's study is but one example of the kind of research project that fits into the model of education as social reproduction. Yet the process by which subordinate frameworks influence the way in which different groups come to relate to the dominant knowledge structure is an area that educational scholarship has only begun to explore, and even Willis's insightful treatment of the lads' working-class subculture calls out for an analysis on other levels.

Willis believes that in their understanding of the world of work, the lads display many insights into the oppressive nature of capitalism. The author calls these insights "penetrations." Penetrations reveal an understanding of the deeper requirements and determining forces of capitalist society. These penetrations do not, according to Willis, provide the kind of theoretical understanding that, through an analysis of the mechanisms of domination, would provide the perspective and strategy required to act on them. To put it somewhat differently than Willis does, the insights that he perceives as truths about *capitalism* are not perceived by the lads in this way. To the lads these are truths about *life* itself. Capitalism, while central to Willis's analysis, is really only incidental to the lads' own understanding. Thus when they observe that someone has to do society's nasty work, or that one job is the same as any other, they are not *intending* to provide a critique of capitalism. It is rather Willis who *sees* these observations as such a critique. To the lads, their observations are expressions about life itself. In other words, they do not perceive their understanding of work as an insight into capitalism, but rather as an insight into the natural law of social organization. What stunts the lads' understanding and enables their own insights to be used to place them on the shopfloor is their own inbred functionalism. This is what in fact limits their penetrations. Willis correctly perceives these insights as limitations. However, it remains to analyze their conceptual source and to provide a critique of their moral authority.

Willis's study is an example of the way in which an analysis of one aspect of the reproductive process points to the need to examine other aspects. His work is not, ultimately, an analysis of the lads' subculture. It is a critique of capitalism and an exploration of the mechanisms that it employs to reproduce class inequality. Yet the implicit conflict between the lads' functionalist acceptance of capitalism and Willis's critique of it provides the material for a different kind of analysis, one that explores the possibilities for a reclustering of the skills available in contemporary society. In other words, educational scholarship requires a critique of the social product of reproduction as well as exploration of the mechanisms, whether cultural or economic, through which reproduction takes place. It is in the development of such critiques and in the reflective consideration of the social possibilities they raise that education takes on the character of a liberal study.

CHAPTER 3

*Praxis, Responsibility,
and the Professions*

Medicine and law have been proposed as the model for re-forming teaching and teacher education by several of the prominent reports that aim to reconstruct the preparation of teachers. While such an idea is not universally shared (e.g., Jackson, 1987; Tom, 1987), our reservations are different from those of many writers. Although critical of prevailing explanations, descriptions, and justifications for professionalism, we do recognize that personal and social interests require the distinctly qualified practice of specially educated professionals who have the kind of competence, autonomy, and authority needed to serve those human interests. We affirm the social value of appropriate professional privilege, and we find that teaching does in fact share the qualities that justify professional status for law and medicine.

The problem with prevailing models for reforming teacher education, however, is that they misconstrue the promise of professionalism. Suggestions of imitating law and medicine have been unconvincing partly because they have reflected a false image of the praxis that we should be able to expect from doctors and lawyers as well as teachers—an image that fails to demonstrate the competence required for the professional responsibilities of serving diverse personal and social interests.

To learn from studying other professions such as law and medicine, we must first see how they have been obscured by the images they have fashioned for themselves. As Metzger (1987) reports, sociologists in recent decades have argued that those self-images "are not objective descriptions, but ideological commercials, designed to promote the interests of their members" (p. 12). Although Metzger himself criticizes the excesses of this revisionist sociology, its major thrust is supported by the careful and elegant analysis that leads Rueschemeyer (1964) to conclude that:

> The core of the theoretical model is identical with the assertions used by the professions to legitimize their claims for maintaining old and acquiring new privileges. . . . The advantages of a recognized professional position seem attractive enough to mobilize all means of power, prestige, and ideology for the acquisition or maintenance of that position, whether legitimate or not. The differential access of these means, however, is strongly influenced by factors other than specialized expertise and importance for core values of a society. One should avoid being misled by the collectivity-oriented self-definition of the professions into separating their analysis from the analysis of social stratification. (p. 30)

The very attributes of professionalism in what are usually considered the "major professions" may be merely incidental, spurious, or otherwise extraneous to the real conditions of their actual existence.

MEANINGS AND VALUES OF PROFESSIONALISM

A common assumption among social scientists is that some system of technical knowledge is a defining feature of the genuine professions. Concern for a scientifically grounded technical knowledge base as the mark of professional status is at least implicitly responsive to the logic of Nathan Glazer's (1974) explanation for why education has been regarded as a "minor profession" (like social work, town planning, and divinity), lacking the essential characteristics needed for the kind of policy treatment that is afforded to the two "major professions" of law and medicine. Glazer suggests that diverse manifestations of lower status for schools of education and the other "minor professions"

> might be reduced to the fact that in some sense these are not "true" professions, that they aspire to a status higher than they possess, and that the base of knowledge and competence with

which students enter practice is not really serious, specialized knowledge. (p. 349)

Glazer does indicate what counts as "really serious, specialized knowledge":

Practitioners of the minor professions do not possess knowledge at the same level of technical complexity and of the same importance to an individual's life as that possessed by the classic major professions, and their claim to professional status and the privilege of maintaining secrecy concerning their professional services does not possess the same authority as we grant to physicians and lawyers. (p. 348)

For obvious reasons, Glazer's article is often dismissed or ignored by those promoting a fully professionalized model of teaching. But while such advocates may be displeased by the conclusions Glazer reaches, their respect for the logic of his analysis can be seen in their concentrated efforts to secure for teaching the possession and recognition of precisely those attributes that Glazer identifies as crucial for attainment of full status as professionals.

For example, according to deans Case, Lanier, and Miskel (1986) of the Holmes Group:

Profession is a term used to designate occupations that require specialized knowledge and a commitment to continuing inquiry to advance knowledge that may be relevant to the practice and service of the occupation. A profession is altruistic in that its first ethical imperative is service to others. (p. 36)

According to the Holmes report (1986) itself:

The established professions have, over time, developed a body of specialized knowledge, codified and transmitted through professional education and clinical practice. *Their claim to professional status rests on this.* For the occupation of teaching, a defensible claim for such special knowledge has emerged only recently. Efforts to reform the preparation of teachers and the profession of teaching must begin, therefore, with the serious work of articulating the knowledge base of the profession and developing the means by which it can be imparted. (pp. 62–63; emphasis added)

The report claims that "the promise of science of education is about to be fulfilled," referring specifically to "the science of education promised by Dewey, Thorndike, and others at the turn of the century," which, they claim, has "become more tangible" within the last 20 years, as "the behavioral sciences have been turned on the schools themselves, and not just in laboratory simulations" (p. 52).

The assumption that other attributes of professionalism derive from the claim to an advanced, specialized, arcane, technical knowledge base pervades otherwise divergent variations of the mainstream theoretical positions in the social sciences. As Donald Schön (1987) relates, the influential Everett Hughes "once observed that the professions have struck a bargain with society":

> In return for access to their extraordinary knowledge in matters of great human importance, society has granted them a mandate for social control in their fields of specialization, a high degree of autonomy in their practice, and a license to determine who shall assume the mantle of professional authority (Hughes, 1959). But in the current climate of criticism, controversy, and dissatisfaction, the bargain is coming unstuck. When the professions' claim to extraordinary knowledge is so much in question, why should we continue to grant them extraordinary rights and privileges? (p. 7).

In his contribution to an important book that uses teaching, nursing, and social work as examples of "the semiprofessions," Lortie (1969) explains the less privileged position of elementary school teachers in terms of the standard observation that "the knowledge and skill possessed by those practicing established professions are recognized both as vital to individual and social welfare and as esoteric in nature." By contrast, he tells us:

> "No one ever died of a split infinitive" is a quip which throws the less-than-vital nature of teaching knowledge into relief. Nor can elementary teachers point to an arcane body of substantive or technical knowledge to assert professional status vis-à-vis the school board or the public-at-large. That which is taught in elementary school is presumed to be known by almost all adults, and teachers have not been able to convince many critics—and more importantly, legislatures—that "methods courses" constitute a truly distinct and impressive body of knowledge. (pp. 23–25)

Lortie's (1975) subsequent analysis has emphasized the need for a knowledge base that is not only technical in nature but also consists of "growing, arcane knowledge possessed by teachers alone" (p. 228). He sees this knowledge as important not only for its instrumental value as technique but also for teachers' ability "to see themselves as sharing in a common 'memory' or technical subculture":

> Teachers' doubts about possessing a common technical culture affect their collective status in two ways: they make them less ready to assert their authority on educational matters and less able to respond to demands from society. An occupation is recognized as a profession in part because people believe that its members jointly possess arcane knowledge on matters of vital public concern; when that belief is held by key decision-makers like legislators, judges, and state officials, they take action to avoid whatever dangers may lie in permitting noninitiates to practice the trade. (Lortie, 1975, p. 70)

Still other perspectives on the presumed knowledge base for teaching undermine the professional status of teachers. Lortie (1975) recognizes that teachers individually acquire shares in the formidable and enduring tradition of pedagogical techniques, observing that these are passed down over generations of teachers.

The theorists have invariably distinguished such "tricks of the trade," "rules of thumb," or "bags of tricks," as "merely 'empirical' knowledge" (e.g., Goode, 1962; Parsons, 1968), or a kind of "craft" knowledge. Such knowledge, these theorists argue, falls short of the more systematic and scientific knowledge of generative principles—including the principles of scientific inquiry itself—that qualifies the distinctive knowledge base of true professionals. Talcott Parsons (1937) explains that the distinctive competence of professionals "has not consisted exclusively in practical skills." Rather, the skills included in such competence are based on "a form of knowledge" which

> transcends the immediate practical exigencies of the particular professional function; it has been knowledge of a generalized character, not only of certain applications of a group of sciences, but of the sciences themselves, their theoretical structures and principles. . . . The ideal professional man [is] a technical expert in the sense transcending special skills. (pp. 365–366)

As recounted by Clifford and Guthrie (1988), this distinction was quite salient at the turn of the century, when education programs were being established in the universities, shortly after the development of the kind of law schools that we have today. Christopher Columbus Langdell, the Harvard Law School dean credited as the originator of the "case method" in legal education, cautioned that "if law be not a science . . . it is a species of handicraft, and may best be learned by serving an apprenticeship to one who practices" (cited in Clifford & Guthrie, 1988, p. 74). As for education, Clifford and Guthrie recount that:

> The eagerly made decision to offer graduate education put pressure on the small store of scholarly or technical literature on the ancient practice of education. A corpus of knowledge had to be attained quickly—to have something to teach and justify the new place of education in the universities. (p. 75)

By 1910, when education schools were producing dissertations on "scientific topics" using "psychological experimentation" and "statistical studies of the organization and problems of schooling," President Lowell of Harvard could write to Edward L. Thorndike that "here was no dabbling with the tricks of the trade that had been the earmarks of the normal school; here was *Wissenschaft* with a vengeance" (cited in Clifford & Guthrie, 1988, p. 76).

Parsons (1968) speaks of "the requirement of formal technical training" (p. 536) as the first among the core criteria differentiating the professions from other occupations. But with this knowledge base construed in terms of broad and even "transcendent" inquiry, the significance of calling it a specifically "technical" knowledge base demands clarification. Otherwise, it could be thought that everything professionals need from any sort of nontechnical education (including liberal studies) would be included in this broad understanding of the knowledge base. If this were the case, critiques of "technically" oriented models for professional education would simply have misunderstood the language that they criticize. It is important to note Parsons's own discrimination between "technical" and "nontechnical" matters and the singular importance of the distinctly "technical" in his account of the professions. Then we can turn to a more general survey of the value that "nontechnical" elements are seen to contribute in the education of professionals.

According to Parsons (1968), for the "applied" professions, the "problem in defining the limits of the professional pattern . . . concerns the importance . . . of competence in culturally defined technical subject matter. However," he adds,

> No social system is only, or even primarily, a field for the implementation of the kind of technically specific goal-interests that can ignore complex interrelations with nontechnical concerns. Hence, the question emerges as to *whether the nontechnical concerns that impinge on the professional function can be more or less neutralized so that the professional expert need not concern himself too seriously with them.* (p. 537; emphasis added)

The ability to "neutralize" nontechnical concerns is used by Parsons (and others following him) as the basis for differentiating among occupations as to their relative degrees of professionalism. He notes, for example, that "the sense in which the clergy continues to be a profession . . . is at least partly equivocal;" and "the central clerical role must be regarded as marginal to the professional system because the 'application' of technical competence is only one part of the complex of its role components" (1968, p. 537). He goes on to state that this same criterion disqualifies those he calls the "intellectuals":

> In the modern world, concern with the expression of moral commitments and with their application to practical problems, social and otherwise, has to a considerable degree become differentiated in the function of ideology and institutionalized as a primary concern of the groups rather loosely called intellectuals. . . . This concern is perhaps even more difficult to professionalize than the traditional clerical role. (1968, p. 537)

Just as Parsons sees the nontechnical moral and political orientation of intellectuals as disqualifying them from full professionalization, so too he sees "artists" as disqualified by virtue of their orientation to "expressive symbolization," which he opposes to "the professional application of disciplined knowledge" in those fields where "the primacy of the values of cognitive rationality is presumed" (p. 539). We can see here how the mainstream functionalist theory of professions is in fact founded on the dichotomy of "instrumental" versus "expressive" role orientations. This dichotomy is also (and *not* accidentally) fundamental to the functionalist explanation of the gender-differentiated roles of men and women in both schooling and the nuclear family (see, e.g., Parsons, 1951, 1959; Parsons & Bales, 1955; Parsons, Bales, & Shils, 1953).

To condense a long and much more complex story: Within the nuclear family, the infant starts out with an orientation to the mother's "expressive" role as the provider of *unconditional* and *undifferentiating* but *particularistic* love. Socialization and personality development are both seen as occurring through an institutionally mediated process of learning how to interact with the father, and then others, all of whom provide gratification in the form of *conditional* and *differentiating* rewards for the *universalistically* evaluated performance of "instrumental" tasks. Schooling plays a pivotal role in the transition from the *consummatory* and expressive female regime of preschool years at home to the *productive* and instrumental male regime of the postgraduation working world, epitomized especially by the technically advanced professional fields. This transition is further characterized by the initial predominance of female teachers in kindergarten and the early grades, gradually giving way to a predominance of male teachers in high school and college.

This model clearly locates the professions in a distinctly masculine sphere of instrumental technique. Moreover, it suggests that even the most awesome technical knowledge base would not qualify teaching as a profession like the others. The pedagogical role is necessarily transitional, requiring teacher–student relations that are always somewhere in between the instrumental and expressive poles, since their very function is to engage students who are not yet ready for the full instrumentalism of relations in the workplace and to gradually socialize them for their eventual involvement in such relations as adults.

"Technical" knowledge and skills are virtually defined as such by their instrumentality; that is, by the fact that they are merely instrumental means for producing desired outcomes. The more "expressive" role of teachers (and especially female teachers in the early grades), however, depends on qualities distinct from the kind of *technical* knowledge and skill that have been seen as the basis for professionalism. The same expressive (noninstrumental and nontechnical) orientation that precludes artists from full status as "professionals" would disqualify teachers as well, especially those in elementary school.

Our complaint is not only against the gender-related inequalities that result from this model, including gender- and class-related biases against teachers, nurses, and so forth, as compared with physicians and engineers. These injustices result from misrepresentations that are more fundamental to the basic functionalist theory itself. It is not just teaching that is misconceived in this account, but the professions generally. In contrast to the account of functionalists, our view is that professionalism *in general* is characterized by the need for a distinctly noninstrumental competence; that is, by phronesis rather than *technē*. This is the competence required for praxis, or the symbolically mediated social interaction that defies analytical bifurcation along "instrumental" and "expressive" lines. Functionalist accounts based on such conceptual bifurcations have misrepresented not only the specialized education and socialization required for the actual praxis of diverse professionals, but also the general public education that those professionals have in common with their clients as a shared basis for their interactive praxis. Just as diverse professional practices depend upon a general education that cannot be reduced to a matter of functionally determined socialization, so does general education itself depend, in turn, on the special professional competence of teachers: competence that cannot be reduced to any graded blending of expressive dispositions mixed with instrumental or technical skills.

Parsons uses the "technical" as his criterion for excluding intellectuals, artists, and the clergy (and, implicitly, schoolteachers as well) from full status as professionals. Even his broadened understanding of the technical does not span the entire breadth of "arts and sciences," or the breadth of the humanistic "liberal arts" disciplines that he and other theorists recognize as an essential part of education for professionals:

> The ideal professional man is not only a technical expert in the sense transcending special skills; by virtue of his mastery of a great tradition he is a liberally educated man. . . . In the great European tradition . . . professional men have been humanistically educated men, men of liberal culture. It goes without saying that the liberal spirit, the love of knowledge for its own sake, which should permeate the special learning of each profession is inseparable from that permeating those liberal studies which have no direct professional application except in their own perpetuation, transmission, and advancement. (Parsons, 1937, p. 366)

Maybe that does "go without saying"; but would it still "go" as plausibly if somebody tried to say precisely what that means, or why anybody should believe it? Of course, it also goes without saying that, in this passage, Parsons's theory reveals its masculine bias; and Chapter 5 shows that this is not merely an anachronistic quibble over personal pronouns.

A central question for us here is how we can identify the value that nontechnical education has for professionals. Until such value is articulated, advocacy of liberal education for professionals resonates with the notion of knowledge that is good in itself but, curiously, *good-for-nothing*. Such a view, along with its corollary that knowledge that is good-for-something is worthless in itself, characterizes the common-sense thinking about knowledge and education discussed in Chapter 1. Such confusion lies near the center of the mainstream account of professionalism and corrodes recent attempts, such as that of the Holmes Group (1986), to restructure the professional education of teachers.

LIBERAL EDUCATION: WHAT GOOD IS IT SUPPOSED TO BE?

Consider, for example, this nostalgic refrain in Sol Linowitz's (1988, p. A52) plea for law schools to "help make the practice of law the learned and humane profession it once was." Linowitz reminisces on his life "as a young lawyer," when "the law for me was truly a human profession" and "also a learned profession. . . . The leaders of the bar were men who read the classics for pleasure, who quoted the Bible and Shakespeare in their briefs as a matter of course." Although we do know that those leaders were in fact "men," it remains unclear what good they ever did, for themselves or anyone, by stuffing Shakespeare and the Bible in their briefs. Linowitz assures us: "They agreed with Thomas Jefferson that 'history, politics, ethics, physics, oratory, poetry, criticism, etc. [are] as necessary as law to form an accomplished lawyer.' They understood what Felix Frankfurter had in mind when he wrote: 'No one can be a truly competent lawyer unless he is a cultivated man.'"

Although their understandings of Jefferson and Frankfurter, and the value of liberal education for their practice, again seem to "go without saying," Linowitz affirms that "those of us who have spent long years in the practice of law know very well . . . that a lawyer's need for a broad education is as great today as it was in Jefferson's time." Assuming such a common understanding among lawyers, he recommends changing the law school admissions test to reward liberal arts mastery; he also recommends that law schools require students to take courses in legal history and courses from the arts-and-sciences catalogue.

In recent years, such calls for enhanced liberal arts preparation have become increasingly common for the range of occupations that might be regarded as "professional," including even such a technical field as engineering (see, e.g., DeLoughry, 1988a, 1988b; Johnston, Zemsky, & Shaman, 1988; Vild, 1984). A great deal of this literature, however, resembles the Linowitz appeal in its eloquent stammering on behalf of nontechnical values that are supposed to be patently obvious, although they are never clearly identified, described, or otherwise accounted for.

Writing for the Professional Preparation Network,[1] Stark and Lowther (1988, p. 1) note that "the education of most college students traditionally has included both liberal study to help develop appropriate values and attitudes and professional preparation to provide technical knowledge and skill." They criticize "most suggested reforms" of college education for tolerating this "schism between liberal and professional education;" but, for now, they have aptly described the most common understanding of that split. Values and attitudes from liberal education are supposed to provide guidance in the proper use of technical knowledge and skills. In education, we recognize this as the ubiquitous distinction between "cognitive" and "affective" domains, which can be easily dismissed as a pernicious repercussion of the positivist dichotomy between "facts" and "values." But the pervasive influence of such thinking requires that we take time to show the difficulties that result for theories that have been proposed as bases for the liberal education of professionals.

Benveniste (1987) uses teachers as a prototypical example of the "altruistic" orientation that is said to characterize professionals:

> The notion that professionals do good to individuals and society differentiates these vocations from other work. It gives

---

[1] The Professional Preparation Network is "a group of educators teaching in the liberal arts and in eight undergraduate professional fields at four-year colleges and universities" (Stark & Lowther, 1988, p. 2).

the professions an appeal of a quasireligious character that has much to do with making some of the professions far more attractive than they might be otherwise. (pp. 42–44)

Benveniste's characterization of professions as altruistic "callings" is surpassed by the authors in Eigo (1986), who describe the professions severally, and together, as more fundamentally religious "vocations to justice and love." While emphasizing biblical and other theological sources, Schaffer (1987) stresses the importance of such influences as they permeate the literature and general culture within which the commitments, consciousness, and character of professionals are formed. Moral philosophers, such as Alan Goldman (1980), continue toiling at more secular formulations of the basis for the exceptional value orientations that are supposed to characterize "professionals."

Instead of claims that the professions are exceptional by virtue of their altruism, however, we now hear more modest pleas for recognition that altruism still motivates exceptional professionals within those occupations. While altruism remains a central theme in the *ideology* of professionalism (Kultgen, 1988), it has become impossible to maintain that altruistic value orientations represent prevailing norms within the professions. It has become easy to dismiss the claim that "professions govern themselves for the common good" as a self-serving myth (p. 135), along with claims that there is some kind of "distinctive professional conscience" (p. 143) and that "professional schools inculcate the professional conscience" (pp. 149–150).

In direct response to Parsons's description (1937) quoted above, Kultgen (1988) comments:

> The notion that a professional education is a liberal one is astonishing. The traditional professions have recognized otherwise. They have been aware of the narrow focus of the training for which they are willing to take responsibility and have encouraged a liberal education prior to entrance into professional training, though critics charge that this is designed [to prepare the professional] for social intercourse with genteel patrons rather than to provide the wisdom necessary for moral leadership. (pp. 150–151)

Bledstein's (1976) historical study and Rueschemeyer's (1964) sociological analysis lend support to the criticism that liberal education might be more important as a means of providing the professional with a distinctive place in the social and economic class structure rather than as a distinctive moral or ethical orientation. Although this undermines the rationale for liberal education as a basis for professional altruism, it does not necessarily pose a problem for the mainstream functionalist rationale. In that rationale, the value orientation of professionals is expressly *not* altruistic (Goode, 1962; Parsons, 1954). Rather, the ethic (according to Parsons) is one in which the nonaltruistic interests of the professional have been "fused" with the functional requirements of society in such a way that no conflict will arise between egoistic and altruistic inclinations.

The functional requirement to reinforce this happy fusion appears to prejudice the liberality of liberal education by restricting the range of values that might be considered, if not reducing "values" altogether to the factual domain of functionality. Instead of a more heterogeneous liberal education in moral values, we now see "liberal education" as a support for the functional ethics that are presumably part of the same ethos into which the student is supposed to be socialized in the professional school. But just as Parsons recognizes the fatuousness of claims to professional altruism, so do the perennial calls for renewed emphasis on ethics in the professional schools bear witness to how slightly the ethics of their students have been developed, either in those schools or in the preprofessional liberal education programs. Examples were provided a decade ago by the law schools and Watergate; now we look to the more recent Wall Street scandals. As reported in the *Chronicle of Higher Education* (20 July 1988, p. A3), for example, after "several graduates of the Harvard business school were prominently involved in Wall Street insider-trading scandals," the school responded by requiring all of its students to take a three-week course on ethics before graduation.

Whether viewed as moral altruism or as nonaltruistic ethics, the value orientation is seen in either of these accounts as something extrinsic to the professional's basic competence in getting the job done. Values enter only as they impose boundaries on the technical means that may be used for the accomplishment of assigned ends, or as they provide direction and guidance for assigning ends that may be technically pursued. They do not, in either case, figure as a part of the competence professionals need to perform their services. The question persists, therefore, as to why liberal education should be thought to have any *particular* importance in the preparation of professionals. If not part of their special know-how, why would either ethics or morality have a greater role to play in the professions than in any other occupation?

The mainstream functionalist answer is that unlike others, who can be controlled by direct supervision and bureaucratic rules, the professional makes most effective use of his or her technical competence when given considerable autonomy in exercising technically qualified discretionary judgment (see, e.g., Beneviste, 1987). Questions about the scope of that autonomy, or the propriety of practices within that scope, are decided by the profession itself as a group, not by clients, supervisors, or employers outside the profession.

But such autonomy is only rational when there is a basis for trusting the professionals individually and as a group. Thus, in his classic formulation of the basis for distinguishing professional occupations, Everett Hughes (1963) declares:

> Professionals *profess*. They profess to know better than their clients what ails them or their affairs. This is the essence of the professional idea and the professional claim. From it flow many consequences. . . .
>
> Since the professional does profess, he asks that he be trusted. The client is not a true judge of the value of the service he receives; furthermore, the problems and affairs of men are such that the best of professional advice and action will not always solve them. A central feature, then, of all professions, is the motto . . . *credat emptor*. Thus is the professional relation distinguished from that of those markets in which the rule is *caveat emptor* (pp. 656–657).

Hughes neglects to observe, however, that relations with professionals involve different kinds of trust, some of which cannot be based entirely on their professions of superior technical knowledge. As Sykes (1987) observes, our "expectation of technically competent role performance" is one, but only one, form of trust:

> The second form of trust is the expectation of fiduciary responsibility, the expectation that service providers demonstrate a special concern for others' interests above their own. Trust as a fiduciary responsibility extends beyond technically competent performance to the moral dimension of interaction. (p. 19)

Sykes regards this as a matter of trusting the professionals to use their technical competence justly and morally, thus distinguishing it from trust in their professional competence itself. Although we agree on the centrality of what Sykes is calling fiduciary trust, we insist that it essentially involves a trust in the nontechnical competence for professional praxis. This is not something extrinsic to professional competence, as it must seem to be when competence is understood in a more limited technical sense.

We recognize liberal education as an essential factor in developing the *practical* competence required of professionals. If it were needed only to inform the moral use of *technical* competence, then it is hard to see why liberal education for professionals would deserve treatment as a special problem. All workers in the labor force have some specialized technical skills, after all, and it is socially desirable for all of them to use their skills ethically and morally. Liberal education should make the same contribution in preparing both professionals and other workers. The *special* claim that the professionals profess as the basis for their autonomy, according to Hughes (1963), is "the claim to know better than their clients what ails them or their affairs" (p. 656). But for Parsons (1954), this superior knowledge is confined to a sphere of "functional specificity," which is itself determined as a function of the professional's specifically *technical* knowledge and skill. Given this perspective, it is unclear why professionals have any special need for liberal education.

One common functionalist response is that the ethical reliability of professionals is more important because their failings do us more serious harm than the failings of other workers upon whom we might also need to rely. Some occupations are thought ineligible for full professional status, no matter how technically skilled, because they are regarded as "harmless." For example, Goode uses this argument in pointing out that "the public sees no way by which the librarian might exploit the reader or the organization. . . . The reader does not feel he can be saved or harmed by the librarian" (1962, p. 20). The harmlessness of teachers has likewise been cited as a limitation on their eligibility, as we have noted in Lortie's (1969) reference to the quip that "no one ever died of a split infinitive."

We regard liberal education as more than a supplemental source of values, norms, or rules of ethics. We see it as essential to the practical competence used in human praxis, a competence that includes more than the technically skilled performance of instrumental tasks. A brief comparative analysis of the professions will show the need for reconceptualizing their practice as instances of praxis that require phronesis, not merely technique.

PROFESSIONAL PRACTICE AND COMPETENCE RECONSIDERED

A variety of occupations have recently been seizing on "professionalization" as a strategy for upward mobility. When activists address members of their occupation, it often sounds as if monetary and status rewards are the very essence of what it means to be a professional. Addressing legislative bodies, however, the same advocates plead that such rewards are merely consequences of the distinctive character of practice in those fields that deserve recognition as professions. Like the social scientists reviewed above, these advocates generally base their pleas on claims about the social need to protect consumers against the quackery of unprofessional competitors who lack the advanced, specialized, technical knowledge base that qualifies the real "professionalized" cosmetologists, mortuary scientists, and so forth.

Since the general tide of deregulation that began in the mid-1970s, however, legislators have increasingly turned a deaf ear to such pleas. Even medicine and law have lost some of their special privileges, following economic analyses documenting unwarranted social costs from policies seen as the anticompetitive practices of self-serving monopolies. In addition, these major professions lost some of their status when judicial analyses concluded that there is no technical justification for their long-standing prohibitions against advertising and other competitive practices, which the courts have now found to be protected by the First Amendment rights of consumers and providers.

In conjunction with the critical analyses by social scientists such as Collins (1979) and Larson (1977) and other social critics such as Illich (e.g., 1980), such public policy developments seem to reinforce the conclusion that, even in law and medicine, "professionalism" is more a matter of special rewards for politically established monopoly power than any special technical requirements for the distinctive practice of those occupations.

This conclusion is further reinforced by the kind of comparative analysis suggested by Nelson (1988) when he asked about the difference between lawyers and computer specialists. It is not clear that the lawyer can claim any greater technical knowledge base, or a technical knowledge base of any greater social importance, than the computer specialist. Such a comparison is at least equally dramatic when lawyers are compared with engineers, who lack many of the most important privileges that distinguish the professions. Some of those privileges, moreover, are retained in full measure by the clergy, even though this is not clearly based on a distinctive clerical knowledge base and even though whatever knowledge base the clergy might claim as their own would clearly not be especially "technical."

We recall that Parsons noted these same circumstances, leading him to conclude that the clergy must have dropped to marginal status, at best. But notice what weird science this is! Attempting to explain professions as a social phenomenon, the social scientist starts with the prototypical examples (clergy, law, and medicine), discovers a defining criterion (technical knowledge) in one of the examples (medicine), and then changes the examples to fit the new "scientific" definition!

The fact is that engineers do not enjoy the kinds of autonomy and authority that have always been regarded as essential characteristics of the professions; and the clergy, at least in comparison with engineers, do have these privileges. Of course, engineers might earn more money and even enjoy a higher social status in many circles. But to go by these criteria would be to define professions in terms of the rewards they have secured, instead of the character of their work; and such an outcome from comparative analysis would simply reinforce the conclusion that nothing really qualifies some occupations for professional privileges not enjoyed by others in the general market for goods and services.

In fact, a more thorough analysis will show that there is a functional basis for professions in the distinct character of their practices, but that this basis is something other than their technical knowledge, which is not actually a distinctive qualification of professionals in any case.

First, we must substantiate a claim that was simply asserted above: that engineers lack the essential privileges recognized for the professional occupations, including clergy. The most obvious example is the professional's privilege against being forced to disclose information learned in confidential communication with a client. This exceptional protection, which shields the practices of doctors, lawyers, and the clergy, is a privilege derived from the rightful needs of patients, penitents, and other clients. It is the client, not the professional, who is entitled to waive this protection. Thus the protection derives not from the professional's technical capabilities but from the client's need for a protected, confidential relationship with a professional whose expertise might not be "technical" in any significant respect.

It could be thought that this is an isolated example of professional privilege, since it specifically concerns protection against exceptional demands, such as a subpoena to testify in court. In fact, the interest at stake receives much broader protection in professional relationships. For example, in circumstances wherein a doctor serves as the personal physician for an individual patient, privileged communication is protected from disclosure to others, including even a bureaucracy that employs both patient and physician. If a company provides a physician to treat work-related injuries, then the injured patient must be able to speak freely about his or her medical history, for example, without fear that the doctor might communicate the information to the employer, who might use it for other purposes outside the patient's control.

Professional autonomy enables the employed professional to refuse even direct orders from an employer, which is surely a distinctive privilege in our private-enterprise economy. In the case of doctor–patient relations, even legislative, executive, and military commands in the public sector can be refused on such professional grounds, and the professional can be vindicated by the courts and by the profession. Of all public-sector bureaucracies, the military is the least restricted in its internal affairs, so the protection of communication between military chaplains or lawyers and their clients provides a strong example of this principle.

Such exceptional privileges are not based on exceptional knowledge as such, as we can clearly see by comparison with engineers. An engineer is answerable to higher management, and to military or civilian employers in the public sector, without the special protection afforded doctors, lawyers, and the clergy. As we can see in such instances as the space shuttle *Challenger* disaster or the defective Pinto design, engineers often lack the established channels or the means available to other professionals for carrying out their responsibilities even, if necessary, against the wishes of their usual superiors. Engineers do sometimes blow the whistle publicly on unsafe product designs or other management-dictated abrogations of proper engineering standards. But when those whistle-blowing engineers are fired for insubordination, the employer's right to fire them is not generally defeated in court, and finding another job in the same engineering field may turn out to be impossible. The responsible but insubordinate engineer might even be celebrated in the press and elsewhere (see, e.g., Boisjoly, 1988) but does not enjoy the kind of established protection that a doctor, lawyer, or accountant would receive not only on the job, but also in court and in the job market as well.

The comparison with accountants is again revealing. The accounting knowledge base is not thought to be more technical, or more advanced, than the engineering knowledge base. Yet when a certified public accountant is hired by a corporation to prepare an audit or financial statement, the accountant's career could be destroyed for *not* refusing improper directions from the employing corporation. In this case, the professional privilege against market and political demands is based on responsibilities extending beyond both the client company and the accountant's own CPA firm. Again, the privilege is based on the nature of the need to rely on uncompromised communication, not on the accountant's specifically *technical* expertise as such.

This point is nicely illustrated by comparisons within the pharmaceutical industry. There could hardly be a more highly advanced, specialized, and technical knowledge base than that required for the manufacture of prescription drugs, which also involves the kind of life-and-death stakes that would seem to meet the functionalist standard of potential harmfulness. Yet drug manufacturing is perhaps the most completely subject to a bureaucratic, rather than professional, form of regulation and responsibility. Like engineers, drug manufacturers can be held responsible for satisfying fully specified technical criteria. In fact, it is their technical character that makes it possible for such criteria to be ascertained and implemented by authorities outside the field of drug manufacturing itself. The pharmacist, or drug retailer, on the other hand, must be relied upon to serve nontechnical needs of the consuming public. The pharmacist must be technically reliable as well, of course, but that in itself would not justify special professional privileges for pharmacists. We also need technically reliable drug manufacturers, but this is a need that can be met through the technical processes of a regulatory bureaucracy such as the Food and Drug Administration.

For the sake of illustrating this distinction, we have drawn the line too sharply and must now acknowledge certain qualifications. Surely, for example, it is not the case that technical procedures are so completely capable of guaranteeing the trustworthiness of drug manufacturers that we would have no need for anything like the special responsibilities of professionals. On the other hand, this qualification itself suggests that professionalism is required precisely at that point where the need for trust is no longer just a technical matter.

More important is the qualification that our comparative *description* of the situation that obtains in different fields does not presume that those different situations are optimal, or even satisfactory, as they exist. We would argue, in fact, that engineers should have the same whistle-blowing privileges as accountants and other professionals. But this follows from the analogous need for reliable communication, not from the type of knowledge and skill needed for the engineer's technical tasks. Engineers have in fact been engaged in protracted struggles over whether their responsibilities, and their corresponding rights and competencies, should be recognized as more fully professional, or as merely technical services subject to the bidding of management and nonprofessional employers.

Our comparative analysis has been presented as a heuristic for illustrating principles elaborated more adequately below; it must not be allowed to obstruct our vision of ongoing struggles, which include not only efforts to establish greater professional responsibility and competence in previously subordinated occupations like engineering, but also struggles to preserve responsibility and competence even in established professions, such as medicine, where they may be threatened. For our comparative purposes, we have so far ignored the potential for erosion of professional reliability arising from more bureaucratic responses to problems of cost control in the public and quasi-public insurance sectors, and from the continuing development of medical services within corporations (Walsh, 1987), the organization of legal services on an unprecedented corporate scale (Nelson, 1988), and other processes responding to political and market forces rather than professional commitments as such.

We are not denying the more cynical historical accounts of the professions as self-serving monopolies, nor do we deny the importance of specialized technical knowledge for the success of those historical mobility projects. Our critique, however, involves more than a prescriptive policy alternative. We see as a descriptive matter the erosion of professionalism accelerated by the inadequate representation of practice as a process that is purely technical, responsible for meeting merely technical specifications. We are also making descriptive claims about the distinctive professional relations that are threatened by these technical conceptions. The quality of such relations in practice provides a basis for professional autonomy and other privileges, no matter how important stories about greed, corruption, and the monopolization of technical knowledge might be for a complete description of the professions as they have in fact developed.

Of course, we still need to make good on the promise to demonstrate both the nontechnical nature of such relations in the praxis of professionals and the nontechnical competence required. To do this, we will begin by observing how prevailing models of practice deviate from actual relationships between professionals and their clients. Those observations will then provide a basis for elaborating an alternative model based on the centrality of phronesis as the competence for praxis.

Models of Professional Practice

It is interesting to note that both the functionalists and their critics have discussed professionalism in terms of the same models of professional–client relationships.[2] On the one hand, there is the "hired gun" model, in which the client employs a professional solely for the technical expertise needed to accomplish the client's purposes. The professional is expected to be concerned not with the client's purposes but only with the technical means for accomplishing them. While the professional may exercise autonomy and authority in the deployment of instrumental means that the client might not have chosen, the client defers to such autonomy and authority on the basis of the professional's claim to specialized technical expertise.

Some see this model as representing a socially functional norm that is more or less approximated in actual practice. Some

---

[2]These models and criticisms are discussed with reference to the general range of professions in Kultgen (1988). For a more thorough discussion, with respect to law in particular, see Nelson (1988). A more finely analyzed typology of functionalist models for relationships between clients and professionals is critically discussed in Bayles (1981).

critics, on the other hand, see it as a false ideological cover for exploitation by professionals who feel free to disregard their clients' wishes. Still other critics, while accepting the descriptive validity of this model, reject it as a lame rationalization for the unethical and socially irresponsible conduct of professionals acting as "hired guns" for their clients.

The same conflict of perspectives can be seen among those who have discussed professional–client relations in terms of another model, one more concerned with "social control." In this model, the professional again provides an instrumental service based on technical expertise; but the professional does so to accomplish only those client purposes deemed consistent with a broader social good. Lawyers, for example, have been depicted as a profession that serves the general social welfare partly by curbing the less scrupulous tendencies of profit-oriented business clients (see, e.g., Parsons, 1962; Smigel, 1969; cf. Nelson, 1988).

Superficially, these models might seem diametrically opposed to each other: One has the professional refusing to serve private purposes that would detract from the general social welfare, while the "hired gun" model eschews interference by professionals in the client's choice of ends. Both, however, share a view of the professional as a *personally disinterested* technical expert, that is, someone who can be trusted to use instrumental knowledge and skill without interposing his or her own conflicting personal interests (cf. Kultgen, 1988). "Professional ethics" are largely concerned with avoiding any such "conflict of interest." The "social control" model also emphasizes ethical constraints on the range of client purposes to be served through use of a professional's technical expertise. The "hired gun" model observes limitations on the range of instrumental *means* that might be ethically employed, but leaves the client more free to choose the *ends*, relying more on an "invisible hand" (such as the free enterprise market, or the advocacy system in law) to derive social welfare from the pursuit of private interests.

In both models, clients rely upon professionals for a disinterested deployment of the technical expertise acquired in specialized professional training. Liberal education seems relevant only as it might contribute to thinking about ethical constraints on the uses of technical knowledge and skill. Such ethical considerations, and the liberal education that supports them, are seen as extrinsic to the special *competence* of professionals, which is the basis for a client's need to trust them in the first place. We have seen that liberal education has also been regarded by the critics as providing upwardly mobile professionals with the cultural capital to mix smoothly with an already higher-class clientele, but this is not seen as a functional contribution either to the performance of specifically professional responsibilities or to more general social interests supposedly served by the professionals.

Liberal education is also understood to provide general communication skills, which are recognized as important in both "hired gun" and "social control" models of professional–client relationships. First, it is important for professionals to understand the purposes that even the most inarticulate of clients might want to communicate. Second, the professional must be able to communicate successfully to clients what they must do to benefit from professional expertise; for example, when a lawyer coaches a client on how to dress and conduct himself or herself as a witness or in a negotiating session, or when a physician prescribes treatment that requires what is known in medical and nursing schools as "patient compliance."

The ability to understand and to be understood and the role of liberal education in developing that ability are undeniably essential. What we deny, however, is that such ability can be reduced to instrumental communication skills or to techniques for deciphering information about the client's ends and for informing the client on how to cooperate with the professional's technical means for accomplishing those ends. The reduction of professional competence to mere technical skill results from such disjunctions between ends and means, which are construed as separate matters only instrumentally related to each other. Such disjunctions permit the division of labor in which an employee or contractor is responsible for selecting the best techniques available to meet specifications that represent ends independently determined by the employer. If the choice of techniques available is constrained by ethical responsibilities to third parties or the general social welfare, this does not change the essentially instrumental means/ends relationship from which these models are derived.

We have noted above that the instrumentalist model does not logically justify the special autonomy and authority claimed by professionals. This model is not to be rejected, however, on the basis of an a priori commitment to defend special privileges; we reject it, rather, because it fails to recognize the essential aspects of professional practice from which those privileges derive. Empirical research on relations between clients and professionals has begun to illustrate the kind of interactive praxis involved in those relations, with reported observations that reflect some of the differences between practical and merely technical or instrumental activity. A brief look at some examples drawn from this research will illustrate the importance of praxis for practicing professionals.

Lawyers and Doctors

Hosticka (1979), for example, has inquired into the "power relations" betwen clients and professionals, negotiated in their dialogical construction of the client's situation and what they should try to do about that situation. Although the professional typically begins this dialogue by asking "What happened to you?" or "What is happening with you?" the ensuing conversation is not just an exchange of information and further questions to ascertain objective information:

> Description of "what happened" or "the facts of the case" can take many forms, more than one of which may have equivalent *a priori* claims to validity. . . . In the case of professional–client interaction, the primary issue may not be what happened to the client, nor what kind of trouble the client is in, but who has the power to say what happened and to define the kind of trouble. (p. 599)

In analyzing conferences between legal-services lawyers and their indigent clients, Hosticka found that the lawyers interpreted their clients' situations in terms that fit them into both the legal system and the lawyers' overburdened caseloads—even though independent analysis of those situations revealed client interests and possible legal strategies that were neglected as a result of those interpretations.

This research might be interpreted as revealing a subordination of the client's interests to conflicting interests of lawyers and of the system. Yet, considering that legal-services lawyers have generally passed up opportunities to practice in more lucrative and prestigious situations, it is not plausible to explain their practice as a self-serving exploitation of their clients. It seems more likely, rather, that inadequate interpretations of the clients' interests are at least partly the result of limitations on the well-meaning lawyers' competence for such interpretive activity. Such limitations on practical competence do not result from personal deficiencies of lawyers choosing to do legal services or public interest work, who regularly include some of the brightest and most talented members of any law school class. Instead, as noted below, these limitations (i.e., limitations on competence for the dialogical praxis of interpreting personal and social interests) have been actively imposed and maintained by political and institutional arrangements that define "poverty law" and "public interest law" as services that call for instrumental or technical skill, rather than interpretive practical competence.

Sarat and Felstiner (1986) observed the interactions between divorce lawyers and their clients, who did not have the disadvantage of forced dependence on legal-services lawyers. Although the interactions were apparently more symmetrical, Sarat and Felstiner also report extensive dialogical interpretation of the case and of the client's general situation. These researchers report that the dialogue also includes interpretation of the legal system and the range of options offered by the legal process. Perhaps more important, they describe what they call the "legal construction of the client," which depends on interpretations of "what the legal process values in human character and what it wishes to ignore, what the process validates and what it leaves for others to reinforce" (p. 96).

In the lawyer–client interactions observed in these and similar studies (see, e.g., Cain, 1983), the professionals are not merely selecting and executing technical means for attaining ends previously specified by clients; and the lawyer's role in the formulation of ends is not confined to refusing work regarded as unethical because of conflicts with some broader social interest. The idea of ethically constrained technical work appears to provide a better model of the practice of elite and highly paid lawyers such as those observed in research at the American Bar Foundation (see, e.g., Heinz, 1983; Heinz & Laumann, 1982; Nelson, 1988); in such situations, corporate clients with more options and more knowledge of the law are seen to have more control over the work of the lawyers they retain from large and prestigious independent firms.

Nelson and Heinz have convincingly shown that elite lawyers lack the kind of autonomy and authority with respect to their corporate clients that had been posited by Parsons and by Smigel.

Their professional services do not seem to include an important role in modifying their clients' objectives, and their practice hardly causes any deviation in the distribution of wealth or power from the general interests of their corporate clients. Yet their professional status rests not on their technical expertise but on their competence in important interpretive and ideological functions that are distinctly nontechnical in nature. The nontechnical competence for professional interpretation of individual and group interests, in diverse and historically changing social and political circumstances, clearly draws at least as much from liberal education as from any more specialized professional training. Moreover, such contributions of liberal education to the competence of lawyers for the interpretive and ideological functions of their profession are clearly part of the "social reproduction" process, identified in Chapter 2 as the scope and subject of "educational studies" as a field within the liberal arts.

The research on lawyers supports our argument that professional autonomy and authority are based on nontechnical competence for practice in interpretive and ideologically significant roles. That research could tempt us to conclude, however, that instead of generalizing a model of liberally educated professionals, it would be better for society to eliminate those privileges and the professional roles themselves. For, as we have seen, it is sometimes the case that the legal profession has helped itself by helping rich and powerful clients transform the system in their interest, while translating the interests of less favored clients into claims already recognized within the system—claims that pose no threat to the status quo. Such tendencies are inconsistent with the universally benign and public-spirited professionalism celebrated by Parsons and, before him, by Durkheim, Weber, Tawney, and Peirce (Haskell, 1984). It seems closer to Ivan Illich's (1980) vision of professionals as parasites who exploit society and dominate their victims by mystifying and manipulating distinctions between real and artificial needs.

The temptation to eliminate nontechnical functions because of their potential for mystification and abuse, however, is itself grounded in the mystifying ideology that claims technical expertise as the sole basis for professional privilege. It denies the more essential role of phronesis, or the competence for praxis—that is, practice that requires accountability on moral, political, and otherwise nontechnical grounds. Ideological denials do not eliminate the need for such practical competence and most certainly do not reduce elite lawyers to performing strictly technical services for their clienteles. Instead, by denying the nontechnical character of their actual praxis, that ideology has freed elite lawyers from public accountability for the politics of their professional practices (Foster, 1986).

The work of Simon demonstrates why legal practice necessarily transcends any limitation to a purely technical pursuit of assigned ends. In "The Ideology of Advocacy" (1978), he demonstrates how variations of the mainstream technical approach (including legal positivism, proceduralism, purposivism, game theory, etc.) have all failed, in various ways, to provide for legal representation of the genuine interests of clients. In a later article, Simon (1980) details how more "therapeutic" counseling and friendship approaches also serve to provide substitutes for the kind of legal practice that would be more effective in addressing clients' real interests. What all of these inadequate models have in common is the promotion of some form of instrumental expertise as the key to "success," instead of reflective critical engagement between attorneys and clients, which might reveal genuine interests that are not addressed by the technical resources of legal process.

The need for such reflective critical engagement results from the client's need for assistance in interpreting his or her own interests and in weighing alternative courses of action. This need should be recognized as a basic feature of relations between clients and professionals in medicine and other fields as well. Davis (1981), in a discussion of legal aspects of doctor–patient relations, notes how the same unrealistic ideology of client autonomy in the unassisted free choice of ends is reinforced, in both medicine and law, by the corresponding models of doctors and attorneys as providing essentially technical service to their clients.

The relationships observed by Davis (1981) are important for our purposes, since they anticipate the possible objection that law is really different from medicine and other more technically oriented professions. Jackson (1987) was drawing such a distinction when he asked:

> Is teaching more like medicine or like law? Do teachers more closely resemble engineers or ministers? More important, to which model of a profession (if either) should they aspire? The Holmes report . . . wants teachers to be like doctors (no mention is made of engineers!) and the sooner the better. (p. 387)

A great deal of criticism has been directed against the established view of medicine as an essentially technical process. In his award-winning study, Starr (1982) shows the historical contingency of the model that has developed in the United States. Reiser (1978) shows how the "reign of technology" in medicine has come to interfere with effective diagnosis and treatment. We would not deny, however, that technical expertise plays a larger role in the work of some professionals than in others. We deny, rather, that their professional privileges are based on the technical need for such expertise. In medicine, technology itself has produced such an unprecedented proliferation of treatment options that the course of action simply cannot be determined as a technical matter; it requires choices that a patient cannot evaluate without engaging in a dialogue with the physician (see, e.g., Bursztajn, Feinbloom, Hamm, & Brodsky, 1981; Cassell, 1976; Israel, 1982). A cancer victim may have several treatment courses to choose from, each involving different trade-offs among such factors as prospects for recovery, time at home instead of in institutions, and avoidance or treatment of pain. The problem of choosing one course of treatment from among such alternatives is essentially a nontechnical one. The patient does need to rely on a professional who can give expert advice on technical factors in the deliberation of alternatives; but the deliberative process itself depends more fundamentally on the physician's nontechnical competence in asking the right questions about the patient's personal and family circumstances, preferences, and values.

Donald Schön (1983) provides a simpler example:

> [In] the reflective practitioner's relationship with his client . . . the professional recognizes that his technical expertise is embedded in a context of meanings. . . . If he is a physician, to take one example, he may urge his patient to stop smoking, but he may also be alert to discover whether, in *this* patient's life, smoking is a way of handling a level of stress that might have other serious consequences if it were given up. . . . In this sort of example . . . there is the recognition that one's expertise is a way of looking at something which was once constructed and may be reconstructed; and there is both readiness and competence to explore its meaning in the experience of the client. . . .
>
> Although the reflective practitioner should be credentialled and technically competent, his claim to authority is substantially based on his ability to manifest his special knowledge in his interactions with his clients (pp. 295–296)

Such nontechnical ability, we would add, is itself part of the practitioner's competence as a professional. What the patient needs is not merely a skilled communicator to help translate technical information. The professional is also needed for the practical competence that comes with years of experience as a specialist, one who has engaged in praxis with many other clients with comparable problems, problems of a kind that each patient might face perhaps no more than once in a lifetime. It is this kind of specialized competence that enables the oncologist to know what questions to ask about a patient's values and family circumstances, to interpret the initial answers, and to follow up with further questions to help the patient formulate his or her own wishes. The patient relies on the praxis of a competent professional for a dialogical interpretation of all the interrelated practical and technical considerations he or she might want to take into account.

Like other professions, law and medicine are engaged in the broader institutional, political, and cultural processes through which diverse practical interests must be interpreted and pursued. This may be most obviously seen in law. Simon (1984) reports the development of "a broader notion of practice than that of the [conventional] professional vision" (p. 500). For lawyers, this reconceptualization "starts with a conventional notion of law practice and develops it in ways that cut across the conventional distinctions between legal and political" (p. 500). Simon refers to the examples of Gary Bellow's "focused case pressure" approach, which "repudiates the conventional distinction between service" (individual case work without cumulative significance) and "law reform" (class actions aimed at rule change) in efforts to encourage small-scale popular mobilization through the coordination of small individual claims focused on local problems (cf. Bellow & Kettleson, 1978), and to "the efforts associated with Edward Sparer to combine law reform efforts in welfare with recipient mobilization" (p. 501; Simon cites Piven & Cloward, 1971, pp. 208, 248–340).

Such reconceptualized modes of poverty law often led to class action suits against government agencies, which produced an especially hostile response from California Governor Ronald Reagan and his close aide Edwin Meese. Among their very first actions in the White House were efforts to kill federal support for legal services or, failing that, to ensure their depoliticization. Again, the Meese position is that lawyers should confine themselves to providing technical expertise in pursuing ends identified by individual clients. Critics such as Simon, Bellow, and Sparer can easily show that this puts clients with fewer resources at a disadvantage, since the lawyers serving wealthy clients practice without such constraints. Beyond their involvement in political conflicts over specific rights and interests, and in the political institutionalization of procedures, routines, and role expectations for the ongoing practices through which diverse rights and interests are interpreted and realized, lawyers also participate professionally in more extensive cultural processes. These processes generate broadly shared cultural interpretations of practical interests, obligations, and our rightful expectations of each other (see, e.g., Macaulay, 1987).

The institutional, political, and cultural dimensions of medical practice may not be so obvious, but they are no less real or important. In hospitals, for example, patients need to rely not only on their own personal physicians; they must also rely on the professionalism of the medical staff, a staff that should operate independently of hospital management to maintain an institutional regime in which patient interests are protected against competing interests, even including economic interests of the hospital itself (see, e.g., Harris, 1977). This is not to claim that such conditions are generally fulfilled in hospitals as a matter of course, but only that the professional responsibilities of doctors, and the required practical competence, do extend to such institutional functions. Patient involvement in medical research presents extraordinary ethical problems, for which technical conceptions of ethical decision making provide no substitute for competent ethical praxis (cf. Veatch, 1987).

The ethical responsibility of physicians can be undermined by limitations on their autonomy within institutions. This tension gives rise to problems in the roles developing for physicians within corporations (Walsh, 1987), as well as other practice settings in which bureaucratic measures are being adopted to expand access to and/or control the costs of medical care. In their opposition to proposals for national health insurance or a national health service, as in their earlier opposition to Medicare (Marmor, 1973), medical societies have claimed to represent the interests of patients and the general public in defending the traditional autonomy and authority of physicians, invoking the sacred doctor/patient relationship and decrying the impending evils of "bureaucratic medicine." Although more cynical interpre-

tations of such political activity by organized medicine seem irre-
sistible, the public interests that the medical societies have
claimed to represent are not so easily dismissed. Such public
interest advocacy is more clearly exemplified by the work of
specialists in occupational and environmental medicine and by
societies of pediatric specialists who have lobbied actively on
children's issues ranging from child-resistant packaging for drugs
and other hazardous substances, to safety restraints for young
children in automobiles, to restrictions on television advertising
and programming during children's viewing hours.

After reviewing earlier calls for physicians to recognize a
professional responsibility to serve as "the natural attorney for
the poor" and to be "healers of social as well as individual pathol-
ogy," Jonsen and Jameton (1977) continue:

> Physicians should be concerned about war, racism, and pov-
> erty, but so should all citizens. Is there some special feature of
> being a physician which gives rise to a set of social and political
> responsibilities of physicians as such? If there are, do they
> create any peculiar problems of ethical conflicts and priorities
> of value for those who bear them? (p. 376)

Jonsen and Jameton explain how they would answer these questions on the basis of a judgment that "there must remain persons
whose primary responsibility is diagnosis and therapy":

> We have thus chosen to view physicians as technicians of
> diagnosis and therapy whose ethical task is to find humanitar-
> ian ways to practice their work, rather than to see them as
> humanitarians in search of a technique. . . .
> We assume that they have the same sorts of political and
> social responsibilities everyone has. . . . The task for physicians
> is to find ways to integrate general and professional responsi-
> bilities. If there is anything special about physicians' responsi-
> bilities for general welfare, it grows out of the symbolic power
> given their acts by the nature of their patient responsibilities.
> (p. 398)

This approach does follow understandably from the modern
bifurcation between ethics and skill, which underlies the mainstream functionalist view of professions shared by Parsons and
others but which is undermined through a recovery of the older
understanding of phronesis as the competence for praxis in

which ethical and technical considerations are not actually divisible. The mainstream modern view of the medical profession fails to account for the special role of pediatricians lobbying on the issues mentioned above. It is simply not true that their position on such political matters is just another subjective value preference, with only a "symbolic power" enhanced by their responsibility for technical diagnosis and treatment. Instead, we see these pediatricians, like other doctors and lawyers observed above, as having special responsibilities based on a political and ethical competence that is inseparable from the phronesis, or the fully practical competence, required for their actions as professionals responding to the special needs of their individual patients and clients.

Advances in medical technology do increase the need for technical skill; but they enhance the need for broader practical competence even more, as an increasing range and variety of technically available options shifts the decision on a course of medical treatment more and more from mere technical judgments about how to postpone and minimize the risk of a patient's death to practical judgments about the quality of life in different treatment regimes (Mason, 1988). These are choices to be made by patients and their families, not by physicians choosing in their place; but the doctor is not merely an advanced technician choosing means to accomplish ends that have been independently chosen by the patient. Instead, the doctor's technical expertise makes him or her the person that a patient depends on for the broader, nontechnical competence needed for the dialogical praxis of formulating choices and assessing them within a practical, or action-oriented, interpretation of diverse and competing interests.

Public deliberation on policies affecting health and health care services involves interpretation of the same kinds of practical interests, though on the social rather than the individual level. In their capacity as specially qualified professionals, physicians have the same kind of special role to play in such policy deliberation as they do in their conversations with individual patients. The practical interpretation of competing human interests involves representation of unpriced "use values" that tend to be obscured by the monetary "exchange values" of the marketplace. It would be naive, of course, to forget that providers do have special interests of their own at stake in such deliberations. Regular providers also have, however, special knowledge of public and consumer interests. These include needs and interests that a provider cannot satisfy by serving clients individually—common or shared interests that can be pursued effectively only through collective action informed by public discourse on political and social responses to the public recognition of such needs and interests. Such policy-related discourse often depends upon the competence of specialized professionals for an interpretation of the interests at stake in the recurring problems they encounter in their practice, which would not be visible, as common interests, to clients or members of the public individually, outside of that public discourse. Such interests can be adequately represented only by those with specially qualified knowledge of the values at stake. Both the freedom and the competence of professionals for such roles in public discourse are protected by the special privileges that differentiate their practice from the more prevalent capitalist forms of operation, controlled by employers and stockholders constrained only by the terms of contracts that have been negotiated in the marketplace of monetary exchange values.

CONCLUSIONS

Parsons (1968) was not wrong in claiming an importance for the privileges that distinguish norms within professional practice from those that would prevail in an undifferentiated capitalist system. His mistake was in characterizing the difference as one epitomized by the technical rationality of engineers, rather than the politically and ethically informed practical competence, or phronesis, that engineers may share with doctors, lawyers, and members of the clergy. The essential and distinctive characteristic of professionals is their involvement in the kind of social and interpretive praxis that requires phronesis, or a practical competence beyond mere technical skill. This view differs not only from Parsons's theory, based on the functional importance he imputes to the professionals' technical expertise and values; it also departs from the even more widespread empiricist and nominalist approach, which devotes itself to cataloging discrete "traits" found in occupations conventionally recognized as the professions. John Kultgen (1988), who also faults both functionalist and empiricist accounts for misrepresenting the true nature and importance of professionalism, concludes his recent study with a chapter calling for "professionalism without professions."

The reformulation that this calls for is advanced considerably, we believe, by an ability to recognize the kind of practical situation that calls for professional praxis and competence, even from those who would not be conventionally regarded as professionals. This implies a correlative ability to recognize situations in which there is no reason for granting special privileges even to members of the established professions, that is, when they are called on to perform more strictly technical tasks for which they can be held accountable without reference to the conditions required for social praxis. The differences between professional praxis and the performance of technically specifiable tasks proves to be the basis for an understanding of "professionalism" and the competence that it requires, without accepting either functionalist or empiricist accounts of current conduct in specific occupations as the measure of the full potential value of truly professional education.

The perpetuation of special privileges for professionals cannot be justified without the development of praxis that actually delivers on the true promise of professionalism: the promotion of values and interests that would not be realized by the arguably more efficient general market for technical skills. Since the promised benefits of that praxis cannot be delivered without the necessary practical competence, an understanding of the nature of such competence must be a first priority in thinking about the significance of liberal education in the preparation of professionals.

CHAPTER 4

Professional Praxis and Education

The examples discussed in the previous chapter illustrate the need for professionals with the practical competence for diverse forms of specialized praxis. The specialized practical competence that they need, however, must be distinguished categorically from their specialized technical knowledge and skill. Despite their familiar pretenses, the essential praxis of professionals is not the kind of unilateral service that experts can accomplish on their own, for the benefit of passively compliant and receptive (to wit, "patient") clients. Although professionals also need the technical skill to perform such services for clients (as when a surgeon operates on an unconscious patient), it is not their skilled performance of those technical tasks that distinguishes professionals from equally skilled high-tech mechanics, whose work might also have life-or-death consequences for the consumer.

Professionals are distinguished, rather, by the kind of praxis in which specialized practitioners and their clients must be actively involved in a dialogical determination of the course of action to be followed by both. Whatever technical skill may be required to carry out the chosen course of action, the choice itself requires a process of deliberation in which the alternative possible courses of action, and the client's practical interests, can be interpreted and assessed in relation to each other. For this, the lay client requires more than technical skill from the professional. Phronesis also is required: the competence for praxis based on sound dialogical interpretation of the personal and social interests that may be involved.

Clients must depend on the professionals to competently formulate choices and pose questions based on specialized expertise in practical deliberation over matters previously unfamiliar to the client. Professional authority does not preempt the clients' opportunity to choose; rather, it enhances the clients' competence to make choices that are meaningfully their own.

Ultimately, this praxis is a joint enterprise. Not only does the client depend on the professional's competence; the professional depends on the client's practical competence in realizing the potential value of the expert's more specialized competence. The competence of a lay client is largely developed prior to the first meeting with any particular professional, having developed over the lay person's entire life of social praxis, including prior praxis with professionals. The specific competence a client brings to bear in praxis with a particular professional, however, will eventually take its specific form within the dialogue of their joint praxis.

The relation is reciprocal but not symmetrical: Each depends on the other's phronesis, but both require competence for a specific praxis, a praxis in which only the professional has specialized expertise. Kultgen (1988) notes that "the complexity of modern life reduces everyone to lay status in every field but one. The physician is an amateur psychologist, lawyer, engineer, accountant, personnel manager, marketeer, etc. and each of the others is in a similar position" (p. 323). The capacity for special forms of practical competence does depend on the more general phronesis of both clients and professionals; in this situation, however, it is the specialist who bears a particular responsibility for teaching and counseling.

Kultgen (1988) observes that "much can be done to prepare people to take part in professional decisions and it is the obligation of the professions to see that this is done" (p. 307). Kultgen develops this theme "under the metaphor of the professional as teacher" and devotes the penultimate chapter of his study to what he calls "the pedagogical imperative" for all professionals. This includes the imperative for professionals to learn from their clients: "Since good teachers are also good students (of the needs and circumstances of their students as well as the latest developments in their discipline), the pedagogic model also represents professionals as learners and those whom they serve as teachers" (p. 308; cf. Schön, 1983, pp. 299–302).

Kultgen (1988) reminds us that in Plato's *Laws* we find questions about the nature of law explained through analogy with the different treatment free men and slaves receive when they are sick:

> The slaves are for the most part treated by slaves. . . . None of these latter doctors gives or receives any account of each malady afflicting each domestic slave. . . . Claiming to know with precision, he gives his commands just like a headstrong tyrant and hurries off to some other sick domestic slave. . . .
>
> The free doctor mostly cares for and looks after the maladies of free men. He investigates these from their beginning and according to their nature, communing with the patient himself and his friends, and he both learns something himself from the invalids and, as much as he can, teaches the one who is sick. (Plato, 1980, p. 107)

As Kultgen (1988) notes:

> Too many professionals treat clients in the manner of slaves or, in the modern equivalent, as machinery in need of service. . . . We must explore the implications of the conception that professional service is an interchange among equals and how it follows that the role of the professional is that of teacher as well as partner and agent. (pp. 307–308)

Kultgen (1988) thus sees the teacher as a paradigm for all professionals. Not only are professionals obliged to serve individually as educators vis-à-vis individual clients; the professions, collectively, must also serve as educators of the general public.

Kultgen notes in particular the "heavy burden of promoting communicative integrity" that is imposed on the professions by their position in contemporary society, observing that this burden "gives the professional ideal the power to contribute mightily to the transformation of society if only it can take hold and first transform professions and professionals" (1988, p. 344). He agrees with us insofar as he proposes an ideal of professional practice based on communication that not only educates the client, but also pedagogically transforms professionals, professions, institutions, and political societies as well. He derives his conclusions from an analytical survey of problems and examples in a broad range of professions; but without the theoretical tradition of phronesis and praxis, Kultgen does not articulate the basic principles for understanding the relationships that he has observed or inferred. Since those principles reveal the nature of the competence to be promoted in the education of professionals, we discuss them briefly in the next section, before drawing implications for the interrelationship of professionalism, educational studies, and the liberal arts.

PRAXIS, PHRONESIS, AND *BILDUNGSPROZESS*

We have departed from prevailing accounts of the professions in our claim that special treatment for professionals is not a functional requirement of advanced technical knowledge and skill. Rather, we have argued that it is a social response to the need for privileged spheres of dialogical praxis that are protected against pressures from the commercial market, which is more than ready to reduce personal and social interests to commodified exchange values. Our approach also identifies phronesis, rather than technique, as the competence required for the kind of specialized practice that merits recognition as the praxis of professionals. Liberal education can now be understood as indispensable for the development of such phronesis, or the practical competence needed by professionals to do their jobs. Liberal education should not be seen solely as a source of extrinsic "values" for imposing ethical boundaries on how professionals use their technical powers or as a source of cultural credentials for their upward social mobility.

The recent upsurge of interest in how the liberal arts can contribute to the education of professionals has produced a number of discussions in which liberal education is recognized as providing subtle and complex thinking and communication skills that are needed for successful job performance, in addition to providing the moral values to help direct how those abilities are to be used (see, e.g., Marsh, 1988; Petrie, 1987; Stark & Lowther, 1988). In these formulations, the proficiencies developed through an education in the liberal arts are still portrayed as cognitive and social skills, or techniques, rather than as elements of practical competence. As we understand these formulations, however, they do not actually reflect a considered judgment that the liberal arts in fact provide merely instrumental or technical skills rather than practical competence. Instead, they reflect the condition of contemporary Anglo-American discourse, from which the distinction between practical and instrumental abilities has all but disappeared (cf. MacIntyre, 1984, 1988).

The fundamental importance of this distinction is, however, recognized by Grundy (1987) as the basis for professionalism in teaching:

> When the work of teachers is informed by a technical interest, the work is recognizable as a manifestation of craftsmanship (or perhaps workmanship). When the practices which foster learning are engaged in a way which is dependent upon the exercising of the practitioner's practical judgments, then that work may be deemed to be characterized by professionalism. Professionalism has its outcome in 'practical action'. (p. 180)

Grundy provides a good introduction to the tradition of understanding that Habermas and Gadamer both share, despite their differences, as an inheritance from Aristotle (see, e.g., Gadamer, 1987; cf. Beiner, 1983). Although, in following Habermas, she might be guilty of neglecting tensions among classical and modern elements within this tradition, such difficulties should not distract us from the more general need to recover meanings and distinctions that have been lost or suppressed in English analytical thought. This obviously requires a project that we can do no more than point to in this book. Yet we do need to indicate briefly the principles within this tradition for understanding those features of actual practice that were noted in our review of the professions, as well as the practical competence that they require. Without some understanding of those principles, it would be possible to misunderstand "praxis" and "phronesis" as nothing more than novel and obscure terminology that can be obviated by more adequate accounts of practice, based on a more complex and subtle analysis of advanced technical proficiency.

The positivist analytical tradition of Hobbes, Hume, and their modern descendants insists upon the separation of "facts" and "values," which prevents an adequate appreciation of the nature of praxis and practical competence. Reflecting the Cartesian separation of body and soul, this dichotomy is replicated in the separation of a professional's technical skill and ethics, of the client's subjective values and purposes, and of the professional's objective command of instrumental means for pursuing ends chosen by the client.

Without understanding the principles that distinguish praxis from the instrumental pursuit of prespecified ends, even modern critics such as Schön, who has clearly observed that nontechnical ability is essential for professionals, are unable to articulate how practical competence differs from instrumental technique. Schön (1983, 1987) falls back on a concept of "artistry," which is supposed to differ by virtue of the more tacit character of its judgments. Even the most tacit knowledge and ability are still technical, however, if they involve no more than the instrumental know-how to accomplish ends that can be specified in advance. There is nothing in the concept of "artistry" that accounts for the competence that professionals need for the kind of practices Schön has illustrated with examples of clients and professionals engaged in the dialogical interpretation of interests and outcomes that only become visible in the course of their joint praxis. The word *artistry* itself can even be used as a translation of *technē*, the Greek word for the kind of ability required for *poiēsis* (or "making"; cf. "artifact"), which was distinguished from *praxis* (or "doing") on the basis of its instrumental use for producing outcomes specifiable in advance.

Of course Schön and others (e.g., Floden & Clark, 1988; Fox, 1957; Light, 1979) recognize that professionals must be trained to deal with clients' problems under conditions of uncertainty. Uncertainty in this sense is seen as an important basis for professional discretion in making judgments on the spot, instead of being bound to follow predetermined algorithms. Such uncertainty is seen to call for tacit artistry and judgment for achieving outcomes that in some sense are not knowable in advance; but, in that sense, these are still being described only as tacit technical abilities. Although uncertainty precludes knowing in advance the outcome of a professional's efforts to deal with a client's problems, these efforts are still technical in nature so long as they are directed to technically conceived problems and solutions. When the professional cannot technically specify the problem, or what would count as a solution, without returning to a dialogue in which those questions are considered as posing new questions for a reinterpretation of the client's interests, then the professional becomes engaged in praxis with the client, calling for a fully practical competence.

Phronesis is the kind of competence required for the practical judgment involved in the interpretation of personal and social interests to guide practical action. This is distinct from the umpire's judgment in calling strikes and balls, which, no matter how tacit in its exercise, is based in principle on fully specifiable criteria. Technical criteria can be specified for judging technical aspects of work by professionals, as Berliner (1986) suggested in his presidential address to the American Educational Research Association:

> Education would be lucky if it could become 10% as rigorous as the judging of livestock, potatoes, poultry, and figure skating. Currently, with annual turnover of untrained, inexperienced judges . . . we can expect an image of teaching that is . . . inadequate to judge contemporary classroom teachers. (p. 9)

Aspects of the teacher's work that could be judged on technical criteria, as in the judging of livestock, poultry, and potatoes, however, clearly do not encompass all important aspects of the teacher's work—especially those that warrant recognizing and preparing teachers as professionals.

Beiner (1983) has explained phronesis as the competence for judgment in political praxis, drawing from the work of Aristotle, Gadamer, Arendt, and Habermas. He explores the continuity of nontechnical competence required for interpretive judgments in politics, in professional and other interpersonal praxis, and even in the hermeneutical and aesthetic practices of persons within interpretive communities. Gadamar (1987) is also very helpful in explaining the Aristotelian notion that a distinct kind of competence would be required both for political action and for the personal interpretation of social and verbal meanings. This notion, that the same kind of competence is needed both for politics and for linguistic or interpretive activity in general, is especially alien to English analytical thinking; but it is presupposed in the vocabularies of Greek and Latin. The Greek *phronimos*, like the Roman *pragmaticus*, is an active, competent participant in deliberation by the *polis* of actions reflecting interpretive judgments of personal and social interests. A citizen without the phronesis for such participation was called, instead, an *idiōtēs*.

Other crucial differences in understanding are reflected in linguistic usage. Noddings (1984), for example, has called for "deprofessionalization" to redress the uncaring ethos she has observed pervading our institutional and social lives. Her plea for caring is articulated in the English vocabulary of "empathy" and "sympathy." As Beiner (1983) notes, however, this is a vocabulary of "pathos" rather than "praxis," of people passively affected by the feelings that they share with others, instead of people engaged with others in the praxis of actively feeling things and acting together. Beiner explains how Aristotle understood phronesis, or practical competence, to include *suggnōmē, eugnōmōn,* and related aspects of the capacity for feeling with other people, but in an active way, interpreting those feelings with a view to judging among possible actions that those feelings might inform. If this can be revitalized in our conception of the competence required by professionals, and developed in their education, then a fully practical model of professionalism might qualify as part of the solution to the problem Noddings is addressing, rather than being part of that problem itself.

The continuity of phronesis as the competence for both the political and personal, for moral action and for interpretive understanding in general, as well as for professional practice, should be more comprehensible in light of the examples noted earlier of the need for referring back to an interpretive dialogue, in which client interests and alternative courses for professional praxis are explored in application to each other (in the hermeneutical, rather than the technical, sense of "application"; see Gadamer, 1982). What makes this so difficult to grasp for modern analytical thinking is the Cartesian prejudice, according to which language is a technical device for expressing, in the external material world, thoughts in the mind of an individual whose interests and preferences originate in the autonomous identity of a nonmaterial soul. This prejudice supports the idea that human behavior is either instrumental (as with objective, technical knowledge and skill) or expressive (as with subjective, ethical values); and in the "affective" domain of values, it supports the idea that behavior is either egotistic or altruistic.

We have seen how both these implications of the analytical prejudice are implicated in the prevailing ideologies, which portray professionals as experts instrumentally applying their advanced, specialized technical skills in serving purposes unproblematically ascribed to the client, subject to ethical constraints construed either as functional norms or altruistic moral values. What these ideologies deny is the process in which individual and social identities are formed within social practices, through which the individuals also come to interpret their own personal and social interests. Understandings of interest take form through the interpretive practices of their signification; they are not in-

trinsic features of prefabricated and fixed personal identities, to
be "expressed" or "instrumentally" achieved. The competence for
such interpretive understandings is continuous with competence
for moral action informed by *suggnōmē*, or the active "feeling and
judging with others." This is not altruism as opposed to egotism;
it is, rather, a competence demanded by the *process* in which people
all *take form* through social praxis.

This "process of taking form" is yet another clumsy translation for a word that has no satisfactory counterpart in English:
this time, the word *Bildungsprozess*, which has a rich tradition in
German thought (Smith, 1988; Gadamer, 1982; Weinsheimer,
1985), although we know it only in our borrowing of *Bildungs-
roman* for literary narratives of education. As Smith (1988) explains:

> *Bildung* has as its primary meaning "education." . . . Its root,
> *bilden* (to form, give form to, to make) connects *Bildung* to a very
> special kind of educational process . . . which . . . can be con-
> sidered the backbone of the Western pedagogical tradition.
> (p. 51)

And, as Shapiro translates (Habermas, 1971):

> *Bildung* means both formation or shaping and the (humanistic)
> education, cultivation, and acculturation of a self-conscious
> subject. *Bildungsprozess* has been translated as "self-formative
> process" in the sense of a personal or cultural process of
> growth and development. "Self-formative" does not imply the
> realization of a plan chosen in advance by the self, but a process
> in which the self nevertheless participates. (p. 320, translator's
> note 6)

With an understanding of *Bildungsprozess*, we can grasp the
underlying continuity of praxis as transformative interpretation
and moral social action, in teaching and in all professional practice, and in the liberal and professional education that plays a
central role in developing phronesis, or the practical competence
for praxis in all these domains. We can begin with the relationship between *Mündigkeit* and *Bildungsprozess*, on both individual and
sociohistorical levels, that Habermas (esp. 1979) has been especially concerned with demonstrating. As McCarthy (1978) explains:

Mündigkeit, literally "majority" (from *mündig:* "of age"), is a central concept of classical German philosophy. . . . The *Mündigkeit* of an individual or group is conceived as the telos of a developmental or formative process (*Bildungsprozess*). (p. 396, note 5)

Progressively advancing levels of *Mündigkeit* can be attained not only in the *Bildungsprozess* of individuals and of comprehensive national societies but also in that of more specialized interpretive communities, such as the professions, the academic disciplines, and the larger professional, educational, and cultural communities within which they are embedded. Linguistic dimensions of the competence required for the interpretive practices involved are variously discussed in Taylor (1985), Gadamer (1982, 1987), and Habermas (1979, 1984).

Gadamer (1982) explains why this is not a technical process, while indicating its significance for education:

> The result of Bildung is not achieved in the manner of a technical construction. . . . Bildung as such cannot be a goal, it cannot as such be sought, except in the reflective thematic of the educator. . . . The concept of Bildung transcends that of the mere cultivation of given talents. . . . The cultivation of a talent is the development of something that is given, so that the practice and cultivation of it is a mere means to an end. (p. 12)

As Weinsheimer (1985) explains: "Bildung means the specifically human way of coming into one's own (*ausbilden*) through enculturation. Bildung is distinct from cultivation in that it is more the acquisition of potencies than the development of latencies" (p. 69). The interests being interpreted in professional or other social praxis include interests in such potencies, which are not given in advance as ends desired by clients with previously fixed personal and social identities. Professional praxis is overtly or covertly involved in the interpretation of such real, but not previously articulated, practical interests. On the one hand, praxis is not reducible to technical production of prespecified ends; on the other hand, truly professional praxis will not interpose the interests of professionals or others (see Simon, 1978) but will assist in the client's interpretation of his or her own real interests. As Weinsheimer (1985) explains:

What the interpreter is—not just what he thinks and does—
changes in interpreting; it is an event of being that occurs. But
this event changes what he is in such a way that he becomes
not something different but rather himself. (p. 71)

Professional practice, in itself, is viewed as an example of this
process in the professional's own life. As Gadamer (1982) relates:
"Practical Bildung is seen in one's filling one's profession wholly,
in all its aspects. But this includes overcoming the element in it
that is alien to the particularity which is oneself, and making it
wholly one's own" (p. 14). This Hegelian formulation (of the
insight that we are destined to become what we do in life) suggests that, like it or not, professionals themselves are formed by
their own practice. Since their practice involves continual transformation of clients, larger societies, and the professionals themselves, we are confronted with the necessary project of developing modes of practice worthy of all those implicated interests and
providing formal and informal education for professionals to
qualify for those modes of practice.

IMPLICATIONS FOR PROFESSIONAL EDUCATION

We can now see how a broad, liberal education is required for
the practical competence of professionals, and not just for high-
level technical knowledge and skill, or for an ethical value orientation seen as something extraneous to practical ability. Also, we
now see that the praxis of professionals is personally and socially
transformative as *Bildung* and, in that sense, is always educational. This supports the argument in Chapter 2 that educational
studies must be comprehensive of the social reproduction process
in general. It also indicates why educational studies cannot be
limited to studies of technique but must engage in open inquiry
as a field of liberal study. Finally, it shows the importance of such
educational studies, along with other liberal studies, in the preparation of professionals.

This suggests a broader role for schools and departments of
education than training future teachers to perform instrumental
tasks. In *Ed School: A Brief for Professional Education*, Clifford and
Guthrie (1988) seem to challenge this broader role when they
argue as follows:

Imagine, if you can, a medical or law school that consciously eschewed preparing practitioners for their own mundane duties; that decided to alter its charter so as to deemphasize its practical mission. . . . There may well be research institutes that indulge in such cleavages . . . but these are not *professional schools*. (p. 329)

In fact, we can consider this possibility without straining our imaginations, as we can see from this statement in the catalogue of the University of Michigan (1986), which boasts one of the top-rated law schools in the United States:

The Law School is very much a professional school. But it is distinctly not a vocational school. Students are not trained to perform many, or even most, of the tasks that its graduates may be called upon to perform as lawyers. (p. 15)

The University of Michigan is not describing any revolutionary innovation here,[1] but simply the ideal of liberal professional education for practitioners that has traditionally been demanded by the wealthy and powerful firms that employ graduates from Michigan, Chicago, Stanford, and the Ivy League. Those firms expect to train their new associates in technical procedures and

---

[1]Here is a more complete quotation from the catalogue section on "Goals of Instruction" (pp. 14–15):

In order to assess the benefits of the School's instructional program, it is advisable for the applicant to take account of its goals. They are not necessarily the same as those of the students. Some conflicts between the goals of students and faculty may be a mark of a healthful and constructive program, provided the conflict does not cause one to defeat the other.

Most students come to the Law School aspiring to be useful, rich, and/or powerful. The Law School is not opposed to the attainment of any of these objectives. . . . But applicants should understand that assuring such attainments is not the primary end of the School.

By reason of its origin, location, tradition, and present sense of purpose, the School is deeply committed to the idea of the university. It aspires to link the quest for truth and understanding to the practical affairs of goverment. Its goal is to bring the whole of human insight to bear on the study of the law and its institutions. Thus, it seeks to share with its students a knowledge of the past and present forms and functions of law, and a sense of wonder about the law's evolution and future development. It seeks also to provide students an opportunity to learn more of themselves by measurement against the sternest challenges posed by the problems of law in our society. . . .

tasks that they can teach at least as effectively in the course of actually doing legal work. They understand, however, that they can provide no inhouse substitute for the fully practical liberal education that is provided for future professionals in the "first-tier" law schools at elite universities.

Of course, the wealthy and powerful firms will continue to interpret their interests as they have in the past. However, if the preparation of professionals who serve less privileged clients is limited to training them in techniques, those clients will be deprived of the freedom enjoyed by those who receive the counsel of professionals with fully practical competence. Different patterns are possible for the distribution of opportunities to develop practical competence among professionals, with consequences for social reproduction that can only be assessed through the kind of inquiry described in Chapter 2 as the domain of educational studies. Educational studies, in this sense, would contribute to the practical professional education of teachers as well as lawyers and other professionals, although it would not focus on techniques for performing classroom tasks.

Owen Fiss (1985), a Yale Law School professor, has written:

> Law schools are professional schools, insomuch as they train people for a profession. But they are also academic institutions, and by that I mean they seek to discover the truth. . . . (p. 24)

It is believed that the range of intellectual experience which the School provides is intensely useful to persons engaged in careers in law. At one level, it is necessary to learn quite a bit about law in order to participate successfully in the School's program. . . . At another level, these experiences enable the successful students to gain a perspective on their field of endeavor which will contribute substantially to their ability to plan creatively, to counsel wisely, and to learn more when more learning is needed. . . .

In these senses, the Law School is very much a professional school. But it is distinctly not a vocational school. Students are not trained to perform many, or even most, of the tasks that its graduates may be called upon to perform as lawyers, and should not expect to be fully prepared to deliver a wide range of legal services on the day of graduation. . . . Our practice-oriented courses and clinics provide . . . only an introduction to skills and a framework for practice which can only be refined through years of experience. . . . Michigan . . . seeks to provide students with the intellectual and theoretical background with which an attorney can undertake a more reflective and rewarding practice. It is felt that too much haste or emphasis on vocational skills, without a broader and more critical view of the framework in which lawyering occurs, runs the risks of training technicians instead of professionals.

> Law professors are not paid to train lawyers, but to study
> the law and to teach their students what they happen to dis-
> cover. The law school . . . is an integral part of the university,
> and by virtue of that membership and all the commitments it
> entails must be pure in its academic obligations. (p. 26)

Although legal studies described in this way can be seen as
analogous to our conception of educational studies, we agree
with Levinson's (1988) objection to "Fiss's somewhat blithe rejection of defining the social meaning of professing law as including
the training of lawyers" (p. 165). In seeking and professing the
truth that we discover in the study of education, we are making
the university's appropriate and necessary contribution to the
practical competence of teachers.

Although our discussion has now come to focus on teaching
in particular, this is not only because we ourselves are professors
of education. Our inquiry has led, rather, to the recognition of
how education is involved in the praxis of all professions, as
Kultgen (1988) observed in his use of the teacher as a paradigm
for all professionals and in the affirmation that "every professional should be an educator." Our understanding of praxis as
Bildung reveals that professional practice is always an educational
process, even if only in the sense of miseducation through re-
strictive distortion of potential opportunities. Insofar as professional practice always teaches, it follows that professional education is always teacher education. There is a need for professional
schools of all kinds, therefore, to promote development of the
teaching competence that their graduates will need in their praxis
as professionals. Also, insofar as the praxis of professionals is
always a joint practice with their clients, it requires the practical
competence for both professional and client participation in that
praxis; thus even general education in elementary and secondary
schools has a role in teaching practical competence for the joint
praxis of professionals and clients.

On these grounds, teaching might claim recognition as the
paradigm profession rather than a "semi-profession" (Etzioni,
1969) or a "minor profession" (Glazer, 1974). Such claims are
premature, however, as Kultgen (1988) observes:

> Unfortunately and shamefully, our educational system falls far
> short of the ideal. The teaching of skills for ends that are uncri-
> ticized, to be used in conformity to community mores, is the

rule. The public, sensing the debasement of the professional ideal in this form of pedagogy, meet the clamor of teachers for professional identity with polite scepticism. (p. 310)

Since the Holmes (1986) and Carnegie (1986) programs are clearly intended to redress this situation, we might be tempted to applaud their designs prematurely. It seems, however, that the Holmes and Carnegie analyses are deeply rooted in the main-stream functionalist understanding of professionalism. This is not to say that members of those organizations would necessarily be committed to the functionalist approach, as opposed to an alternative understanding that might be proposed. Insofar as our investigation might contribute such an alternate understanding of professionalism, it could itself be seen as an example of the interpretive and dialogical praxis we have been describing.

The Holmes Group (1986) recognizes that "creating and sus-taining a communal setting respectful of individual differences and group membership, where learning is valued, engagement is nurtured, and interests are encouraged require more than a set of identifiable skills" (p. 54). Their report proposes that the required "dispositions, values and ethical responsibilities" should be inte-grated with the knowledge and skill components of a "compre-hensive plan for teacher preparation" (pp. 50–51), but the differ-entiation of knowledge, skill, and value has already precluded recognition of phronesis, or the practical competence in which such elements cannot be analytically distinguished.

The "comprehensive plan" also includes, as one of its compo-nents, "the study of teaching and schooling as an academic field with its own integrity":

Studies of education as a discipline provide a description and explanation of the phenomenon of schooling itself—its devel-opment, its purpose, and the micro and macro mechanisms that make schooling possible and sustain it. A sound study of educa-tion . . . would provide a way of understanding schooling in the same way that the study of any discipline illuminates a set of phenomena. In this sense, education is one of the arts and sciences since it applies tested modes of inquiry to a phenome-non of universal scope and significance. (p. 51)

Paradoxically, this formulation restricts educational studies to the limited domain of "schooling," as opposed to the more universal scope and significance of education, or *Bildung,* as it operates throughout processes of social reproduction (cf. Chapter 2, this volume; Feinberg, 1987); at the same time, it provides no indication of how this component of professional education would contribute to the teacher's competence for practice within "schooling" itself. In the report's own vague equivocation, "while the determination of the origins, purposes, and mechanisms of schooling is vital, the heart of the matter is the structure of knowledge and what knowledge is of most worth" (Holmes Group, 1986, p. 51).

Competence for "imparting subject matter" would be developed, rather, in two other components, which recapitulate the analytical separation between curriculum and instruction: first (curriculum), the "knowledge of the pedagogy of subject matter—the capacity to translate personal knowledge into interpersonal knowledge, used for teaching," and second (instruction), "the skills and understandings implicit in classroom teaching—creating a communal setting where various groups of students can develop and learn." The use of these abilities is oriented, not surprisingly, by an additional component, which "consists of the dispositions, values and ethical responsibilities that distinguish teaching from the other professions" (Holmes Group, 1986, pp. 51–54).

Although the description of these components reveals an interest in pedagogy as praxis, their analytical articulation binds them to a functionalist understanding of expertise and responsibility. This can be seen, especially, in the separation between curriculum and instruction, and in the division of responsibility for knowledge of the subject matter itself (which is identified as knowledge of extant arts and science disciplines) and pedagogical knowledge of how that content matter can be translated in teaching it to students. The functionalist understanding is also reflected in the analytical separation of "dispositions, values and ethical responsibilities" from instrumentally effective "knowledge" and "skills."

As acknowledged in the Holmes Group (1986) report:

> The unique educational matter, not in the domain of any affiliated discipline (namely, the behavioral sciences, history, and philosophy) is curriculum; yet this is one area about which we have little compelling information and theory. Education is the discipline of the disciplines. (p. 51)

Yet the report would preempt teachers' professional curriculum responsibilities by presumptively defining subject-matter content for the schools, as when future teachers are described as majoring in academic disciplines that are supposed to constitute "the subjects they will teach" in school (see, e.g., pp. 16–17).

This suggests, for example, that courses on "political science" would be taught in the high schools—instead of courses on politics and government, which would be informed by several sources, including political science, without being defined by any one of them. Clifford and Guthrie (1988, p. 349) report John Best's observation that the academic political scientist is "concerned with building the discipline" rather than preparing students for participation in politics or government (cf. Levinson, 1970; McWilliams, 1970). Clifford, Guthrie, and Best were careful to distinguish academic from professional school functions, but these are both distinguished by the functionalists from general education as well (Parsons & Platt, 1973).

For another example, we can look to the field of history, where Hamerow (1987) has reported cultural consequences of constricting historical thought and writing within limitations of the academic discipline. Educational consequences are reported by Kozol (1986), who was told by twelfth-grade students that history is a study of past events and inevitable processes that could never be affected by anything that anyone like them would ever do in their own lives. Is this what the school subject of "history" is supposed to teach? Apparently so, according to a poster in the corridor that described history as a field of interest for future historians, archaeologists, and curators, but did not suggest that students might be interested as potentially knowledgeable participants in history.

The Holmes Group (1986) report blithely reiterates the venerable Sputnik-era diagnosis that the problem for curriculum and teachers' subject-matter knowledge is one of fidelity to the academic disciplines. It idealistically identifies the disciplines as constituted by our most authentic knowledge of the domains that they address and views the role of professional teachers as one of pedagogically translating that authenticated knowledge for the students. It thus ignores the more realistic understanding that the academic disciplines themselves function as professions, with all the attendant limitations and qualifications on their practice (Clark, 1987; Toulmin, 1972).[2]

In their responsibility for curriculum, teachers need to be more than flexibly skilled pedagogical translators. For the joint dialogical praxis of interpreting the subject matter in relation to their students' personal and social interests, teachers need the competence for praxis as active, critical clients of the professionals in academic disciplines. How well they serve their students' interests, in relation to the subject matter, will depend on their competence in both client and professional roles. Thus the teacher's pedagogical praxis also provides a more general model, one in which students can see possibilities for critical praxis by professionals and clients in relation to specialized knowledge and expertise of all kinds. This is one more way that all teachers are involved in education for professional practice of all kinds; and, in this case, it is especially through their own professional responsibility for liberal education.

Thus we see how professional and liberal education depend on educational studies for an understanding of the complex and subtle ways that they are dependent on each other. We have also seen how the kind of praxis that is required in education should fully qualify teachers as professionals, not because of how they score on functionalist or empiricist checklists of the "traits" shared by other occupations, but because of the critically interpretive social competence that should be epitomized in teaching and that is necessary, moreover, for real praxis in any profession.

In his defense of the professional ideal, Metzger (1987) affirms his belief "that every desire to enoble [sic] work should be

---

[2]Hence, a distinct field of educational studies is important partly to preserve possibilities for understanding education in ways that might not be supported by any of the other liberal arts disciplines for reasons of their own internal definitions of scope, method, and so forth. Scholars involved in the Holmes and Carnegie movement, for example, actively use findings and insights on schooling and on the professions derived from the work of researchers who have lost academic jobs, not because anyone doubted the quality of their work or its importance and validity for understanding the domains under study, but for reasons pertaining to the self-definition of the disciplines constituted as academic professions. Examples include Paul Starr (sociology) as well as Samuel Bowles and Herbert Gintis (economics). If the propriety of self-constitution by the academic disciplines is recognized, it does not follow that the universe of scholarly inquiry, policy discourse, and general education in the school subjects should be confined within the limits they impose on themselves.

encouraged" and that it is only "when workers no longer give a damn whether they are or are not part of a profession, that there is cause to take alarm" (p. 18). After observing that those who defend professionalism are seen by most sociologists as "guardians of an empty shrine," Metzger (1987) notes that some sociologists of education are now going against that tide of disbelief in their support for current efforts to improve education through the professionalization of teaching (pp. 12; 18, note 1). Metzger cautions us, however:

> It is still too early to tell whether their affirmation of the redemptive power of professionalism presages a wide attack on the true unbelievers or . . . a limited resurgence of faith in an occupation particularly susceptible to paradisiac promises of higher status, or just another pendulum swing in the unending debate over how a mass education system may be brought to a qualitative state of grace. In any event, these sociologists confront the irony of seeking admission to a church at a time when the weight of its theology says that God is dead. (1987, pp. 12; 18, note 1)

We do not mourn the passing of the functionalist's god; nor do we share Metzger's nostalgia for the ineffable nobility of a self-aggrandizing professionalist mystique. Our understanding of the requirements for praxis leads us to affirm a professional ideal for teachers. With that understanding, however, we can reject the view of teachers as the kind of livestock or poultry that some would have us learn how to judge, but without acquiescing, as Metzger ends up doing, in the angelic pretenses of professionalist ideologies. In the tradition of *Bildung*, praxis, and phronesis, we see the need for teachers and other professionals to be engaged in actions that serve our personal and social interests in becoming fully human beings.

CHAPTER 5

Patriarchy and Teaching:
Re-Visioning the Profession

We have argued that to reject education as a field of academic inquiry, as an object of critical reflection, is to mistake the educational enterprise. The practice of teaching conceived as praxis demands an understanding of education as the heart of liberal inquiry. To insist that studies in the liberal arts embody a contemplative purity unsullied by the exigencies of choice and action is to misconceive the liberal arts. John Dewey (1916) once said that all philosophy is the philosophy of education. We cannot agree more strongly as we try to understand liberal inquiry as centrally implicated in the practice of teaching. The need to understand teaching as profession is real and urgent, but it must be motivated by something more than a push for institutional legitimacy. If we accept the boundaries of understanding the profession of teaching as these have been defined within present institutional contexts, we do it immeasurable harm. Nothing less than a radical reconstruction of our understanding of professional and liberal arts study will serve the interests of developing an educational praxis. And nothing less than a radical interrogation of civilization itself will serve that aim. In this chapter we attempt such an interrogation through an examination of the *Bildungsprozess* that recounts the tale of domination inherent in the distinctions we have so far criticized.

Questions of professionalization and professionalism seem to arise when two conditions obtain: when practitioners in the field in which those questions are being debated find themselves under external attack, and when those practitioners are themselves suffering anxiety about their own membership in a coherent, identifiable community. The response to external attack results in a proliferation of articles first asking whether that field is a discipline and then demonstrating that it is by (1) pointing to the existence of what is sometimes called a sociointellectual community (that is, people who consider themselves colleagues, write letters to each other about their common work, work in departments together, and read the same journals and books) and (2) pointing to a body of knowledge and skills unique to the enterprises that constitute that field. We deal with our anxiety most often by engaging in internal debates over methodology, standards, and criteria of judgment. That we are in a phase of response to those two conditions in the field of education is clear from an examination of the tables of contents of journals, publishers' catalogues, and conference programs.

At the present moment, those of us involved in teacher education at liberal arts institutions feel under double attack. Periodically, our colleagues in the academic departments take it into their heads to wonder whether a department such as education has any place in an institution consecrated to the liberal arts tradition. There is no place in that tradition, they tell us, for professional preparation. At the same time our colleagues in large graduate schools and in public institutions question whether we have the skills and the resources to offer adequate professional preparation. Our liberal arts colleagues receive strong support in their campaign against education departments from within our own field: from the research of those who expose the poverty of teacher education programs and from those who argue that good teaching is simply a matter of mastery of the canon in some field and the ability to communicate—nothing, they say, that can be taught in education courses. In response, such reports as that of the Holmes Group (1986) and the current proposal for the restructuring of teacher education in New York State insist that there exists a specific and definable body of knowledge and level of skill that can be provided only by a professional faculty of education. In addition to the fact that such responses will preclude entry into the field by those who cannot afford a fifth year of study, they also betray those impulses and commitments that draw people into the profession—impulses toward and commitments to the practice of the liberal arts.

It should be noted that in the field of education we do more than simply prepare teachers for the public schools. Many of us are engaged in studying the processes and institutions of education in the same way that our colleagues in other disciplines study the processes and institutions of their fields. One of the authors teaches at a university that offers a major in education distinct from the teacher education program, a major structurally similar to majors in other departments. Some even argue that education can be conceived as a field of liberal study only if it is disengaged from the preparation of teachers. That any tension should be perceived between liberal studies and professional preparation reveals a crisis larger than the problems in the field of teacher preparation and its relationship to undergraduate liberal arts studies.

The current debates in the field of education coincide with a recently renewed interest in altering or creating general education programs, sometimes referred to as core curricula. Usually these programs consist of some sort of sequence of courses intended to provide students with a common intellectual experience. This common intellectual experience is most often an experience with *the* "cultural heritage." Our renewed concern for the cultural heritage must be understood as part of a larger crisis in Western civilization, as that crisis is articulated by Allan Bloom (1987) and E. D. Hirsch (1987), among others. As we argue here for a reconstructed notion of liberal and professional education, we are encouraged by faculty members, such as those at Stanford, who would have us critically interrogate and reconstruct the "cultural heritage" of Western civilization in our institutions of higher education (Mooney, 1988).

MODERNITY, REALISM, AND EDUCATIONAL STUDIES

The current interest in and commitment to general education emerges as part of the contemporary response to what we might call the crisis of modernity. Marx's (1848/1967) description of modern life more than a hundred years ago resonates all the more insistently today:

> Constant revolutionizing of production, uninterrupted distur-
> bance of all social conditions, everlasting uncertainty and agita-
> tion distinguish the bourgeois epic from all earlier ones. All

fixed, fast-frozen relations, with their train of ancient and
venerable prejudices and opinions are swept away, all new-
formed ones become antiquated before they can ossify. All that
is holy is profaned, and man is at last compelled to face with
sober sense, his real conditions of life, and his relations with his
kind. (p. 35)

Contemporary intellectuals are preoccupied with what we
now think of as the postmodern predicament—a paradoxical
sense that human beings feel themselves at once cast adrift in a
seismic universe and besieged and beleaguered by unseen and
unknowable forces. Totally free and hopelessly confined, nothing
is certain but change, and as Marshall Berman (1982) puts it:

We don't know how to use our modernism; we have missed or
broken the connection between our culture and our lives. . . .
Our century has nourished a spectacular modern art; but we
seem to have forgotten how to grasp the modern life from
which this art springs. (p. 24)

Christopher Lasch (1984) describes the postmodern predicament as one in which the self, personal identity, has become
problematic and in which the world itself ceases to have substance. We live lives out of our control in a world that "defies
practical understanding." We live without a sense of the past and
bereft of a future. Our failure to acknowledge the claims of the
past and the future on us makes the very notion of moral and
political choice a travesty. The discourse of general education
echoes the anxieties threaded through the criticisms of teacher
preparation.
    The crisis of modernity or the crisis of Western civilization is
seen on all sides—by conservative, radical, and liberal critics
alike—to be disclosed by an intellectual poverty related to moral
paralysis. We live in a world of public lies and private confusion.
And the world at hand is the business of education. The getting
and the giving of an education is a moral project and the pedagogical relationship, a moral one. Our education must bring us face
to face with the question of how one ought to live one's life. Our
education ought to bring us face to face with the consequences of
that response. Our education ought to bring us face to face with
our collective past and with images of our future. Ultimately
educating is about transforming persons, in terms both of their

relationship to the content of study and their relationship to the world in which they live. These two relationships are specular. People have thought so since Plato; it is only relatively recently that the moral imperative of education has been effaced, that our sense of a project has atrophied, along with our capacities for joy and sorrow. In the place of projects, we have short- and long-term goals; in the place of joy and sorrow, we have satisfaction and dissatisfaction.

In our bureaucratized world of regimented mass consumption, a world in which education is seen only as providing access to the upper levels of a social and economic reward structure, education ceases to be a use value. It is reduced to its exchange value, a commodity in a competitive system of market relations. We men and women become commodities, but unlike other commodities, we willingly take ourselves to market. When the prevailing mode of social relations is based on the exchange of commodities, alienation is the standard mode of existence. Perhaps the real tragedy of postmodern existence is that we no longer experience our alienation as alienation. We know only a vague anxiety experienced as dissatisfaction. Our contemporary literature is a literature of dissatisfaction; it reveals a world in which people no longer search for meaning in their lives but rather lose themselves in brandnames, choosing a style over a life.

Many students today describe themselves as realistic. Being realistic consists, for all too many of them, in choosing courses and majors with a view to their marketability; it consists in facing unsentimentally the fact that some people have to be at the bottom; it may even consist in denying that the existence of the homeless, the politically disenfranchised, the starving, and the spiritually dispossessed are blots on the conscience of humanity; it consists in an amused tolerance of the "idealism" of certain philosophers and artists. ("That's fine in theory but it can't work in the real world.") And it consists, paradoxically, in a refusal to confront the possibility of the annihilation of this planet.

Meaninglessness defines too many lives. Meaninglessness proceeds from a negative act of will. It proceeds from an inability, if not a refusal, to engage the world cathectically, a refusal of consciousness to intend. We hear reports of students who have never read for pleasure, have never *chosen* a book, have never had the sense that a book has chosen them. They do not read with a sense of personal urgency, as if on a quest to find themselves through language, through conversation with others. A group of

students reading *Memoirs of a Dutiful Daughter* for a course expressed either bewilderment or cynical disbelief at Simone de
Beauvoir's description of her adolescent self weeping over *The
Wanderer*. They have never felt the passionate pull of ideas and
experiences not their own. Theirs is a culture of information, a
culture in which language detaches itself from things, is used to
veil rather than to dislose, to distance rather than invite. Theirs is
a culture in which truths can become "inoperative" and information become "disinformation." We live in an age, to borrow from
Wittgenstein (1953/1968), in which our senses are bewitched by
language, a language drained of all personal meanings. The trick
is to learn the trick—the trick of the sort of detachment made
possible only by ignorance. We see here a failure of liberal education, not traceable solely to educational studies or to the poverty
of teacher education.

From fiction and history both, we know of the dangers to
human dignity—including now the threat to human existence
itself—posed by ignorance and by a monopoly of a few on the
manipulation of symbols. It has always been in the interest of
tyrants to prevent the development of self-consciousness, of
human consciousness, in oppressed groups. Frederick Douglass's
(1845/1982) wise master, Mr. Auld, knew that it was unsafe to
educate a slave:

> A nigger should know nothing but to obey his master—to do as
> he is told to do. Learning would *spoil* the best nigger in the
> world. "Now," said he, "if you teach that nigger how to read,
> there would be no keeping him. It would forever unfit him to
> be a slave. He would at once become unmanageable, and of no
> value to his master. As to himself, it could do him no good, but
> a great deal of harm. It would make him discontented and
> unhappy." (p. 67)

It was not simply the skill of reading that Mr. Auld was
talking about, but the consciousness and power that come with a
mastery of language, the enlargement of imaginative possibility
that precedes action. The goals and content of general liberal
education have been selected with a view toward helping students to develop those critical and imaginative capacities that are
the precondition of human freedom and autonomy.

It is difficult to imagine a compelling or even informed argument against the value of a liberal education, whatever disputes

may arise regarding the appropriate (to what?) paradigm within which to conceive it. At the most general level, we believe that any practice or experience worthy of the name education is liberal education, is practice or experience that liberates the creative intelligence in service of the imaginative creation of possibility. We believe that the liberated creative intelligence pursues the highest potential of human culture through action grounded in and embodying objects of reflection and contemplation. We believe that through reflection and contemplation we come both to know ourselves as creatures with a claim on the world, a stake in it, and to know the world through its claims on us.

So far, it probably sounds as if we are retracing the picture of education and teaching as seen from the lofty perspective of the citadels of higher learning. That shows that it is possible to perceive the same crisis while arriving at different diagnoses. Position or perspective makes all the difference. We see the world in the same way. We understand it differently. Which is to say that finally we see it differently. Our position is not even in the same universe as that of the Blooms or the Bennetts or the Hirsches. We look to the impulse to domination, an impulse that the feminist literature expresses in terms of the imperatives of patriarchy. For feminists, the logic of patriarchy entails the crisis of modernity. The logic of patriarchy is the logic of exchange and domination. Its logic entails powerlessness and voicelessness. Contemporary reform proposals that sort studies into liberal and professional, foundational and supplementary, obey the imperatives of patriarchy.

The search for foundations has been the defining activity of Western philosophy—a search for that beyond which we need not go and a search for that which will allay our mistrust of our mediations of reality. This search, Derrida (1976) says, is the expression of logocentrism. In a logocentric universe, the world is cut up into series of oppositions: mind/body, meaning/form, nature/culture, male/female, and so forth. In this universe, the first term is superior and belongs to logos; the second is a manifestation or completion of the first. The term belonging to logos is the foundation. Conceived as an opposition—liberal arts/professional studies—the liberal arts are foundation, logos. This logical economy neglects its own peculiar irony, and this is finally its own undoing. If the second term, in our case professional studies, completes the first (liberal arts), then we must acknowledge that the liberal arts are peculiarly dependent for their existence on professional studies. We relate this claim to Derrida's reading of Rousseau. Rousseau (1762/1979) argued that nature was foundation and education supplementary to nature. In the opposition nature/education, then, nature is the superior term. We can relate this to Bloom's (1987) criticism of feminism. Feminist studies are an abomination because they are not built on nature. Legitimate education completes nature. Feminist studies thwart rather than complete nature. Legitimate education enables human nature to emerge as it naturally is. This means, though, that there is an original lack in nature. It means that education is an essential condition of nature.

Similarly, the logic of foundational and professional studies entails a suspicion that the profession may prove foundational to the foundation. The terms of a logocentric opposition may always be reversed, or disrupted (Culler, 1982). Educational studies conceived as a branch of liberal learning is the critical study of paradigms of liberal education and of the reciprocal claims of us and our worlds. Educational studies are a place from which we might move to disrupt the hierarchical oppositions that form the logic of domination and alienation out of which the contemporary cultural crisis emerges. In a sense, educational studies ought to inform and transform our understanding of the liberal paradigm. At the least, that such study ought to be at the center of teacher preparation is clear from the moral nature of the enterprise.

CIVILIZATION AND FEMINIST NARRATIVES

Our civilization is embedded in a logocentric universe. Our education, whether liberal or professional, reinstitutes in each generation the traces of logocentrism. Because a logocentric logic is a logic of domination, the civilization enacted in that logic is a civilization of domination. That civilization, *the* "cultural heritage," is problematic outside of the assumptions of logocentrism may be a source of intellectual renewal (Graff, 1987, especially pp. 1–15).

We want to look at the pictures of education and civilization that have been developed with new eyes, with vision informed and transformed by feminist theory, a theoretical practice that disrupts practices of domination and alienation. It is probably possible to see feminist theory as an attack on liberal education, as even "anti-intellectual." If we understand the educational project in that way, it is likely because we take (metonymically, dream-like) a particular paradigm of liberal education as the whole of liberal education, and a particular syntax as the only language structure. It is time that we wakened from this dream. The process of awakening might well begin with a critical analysis of Freud's (1930) assumptions regarding women and civilization:

> Women soon come into opposition to civilization. . . . Women represent the interests of the family and of sexual life. The work of civilization has become increasingly the business of men, it confronts them with ever more difficult tasks and compels them to carry out instinctual sublimations of which women are little capable. . . . Thus the woman finds herself forced into the background by the claims of civilization and she adopts a hostile tendency towards it. (pp. 51–52)

The university is the embodiment of civilization, or at least of a certain idea of civilization. It is an idea of civilization in which all of its particular values and ideas make claim to enduring if not eternal supremacy. The particular ideas subsumed within the master idea are well known. By now we have heard all of the arguments of interest, ethnocentricity, and so forth. And yet the idea/ideal (*eidos/eidōlon*) remains undisturbed. This is a curious fact in light of the considerable efforts of feminist scholars, scholars of color, and others over the past two decades to reform the disciplines at the core of the university. It must be that the university, the idea of the university, is something more than the media of communication it claims, for otherwise the idea/ideal would by now have been supplanted.

This civilization is as hostile to women, and to all other Others, as Freud claimed women (all of whom he took for mothers) are to it. All educational theory has taken as its center the project of cultural transmission, which we want to redefine as social reproduction. Women's relation to education and educational thought is plagued with disruption and difficulty when, as had been the case long before Freud thought of it, culture is associated with productive labor in the public sphere to which mothers must relinquish their children (sons) and in which children (sons) are to be compensated for the loss of their mothers.

In her textu(r)al weaving of the scene of conversation in which we might locate some educational theorists, Jane Roland

Martin (1985) notes a peculiar tension between the claims of reproduction and the imperatives of production. Martin argues that women have been neglected in educational thought because they have been associated with the reproductive processes of culture, which have been progressively disvalued. By "reproductive processes" (and by now we hope that this would go without reiteration), we mean more than conception and birth; we mean childrearing and those household activities directed toward the reproduction of labor power and the transmission of culture as well as activities carried on in the community that serve to sustain and maintain it. By "reproductive processes" we refer to certain emotional as well as physical and intellectual labor—and it is women who have been largely responsible for the emotional work of our culture, even while emotional work has been ignored. Women are permitted to be the minders of culture but never its creators. Martin (1985) denies that the impulse to nurture is any more natural than the impulse to reason, and she urges us to a view of education that stresses conversation over debate, connection over separation, and rapprochement of "civilization" to reproduction. Work such as Martin's disrupts the apparently stable opposition of production/reproduction.

Women and women's work are associated with nature and with wordlessness. Because women bear children, they are considered "naturally" nurturing. Because nurturing is taken as natural, it is not valued, and because those jobs in the public sphere with which women are most often associated, such as nursing and elementary school teaching, require substantial investments in nurturing, they also are not valued. When, as happens now with increasing frequency, women aspire to and attain positions typically associated with men, they are put in a most peculiar position. Those women who teach in the public spaces of the university may be among those most peculiarly situated, for the culture that we produce and reproduce requires our complicity in our own devaluation and exclusion; it requires of women that they take as their own our culture's hostility toward the feminine. That has been a principal insight among contemporary feminists and what distinguishes us from our Victorian mothers.

As we hinted in the first chapter of this work, since the Enlightenment, the educational project has been assimilated to a gentlemanly search for a rational basis for human conduct and decision making. In the search for a rational basis, all of those sentiments, dispositions, and characteristics we have come to associate with the feminine have been relegated to the margins. In the oppositions masculine/feminine, male/female, the superior term is obvious. We might go so far as to say that all of those things that could not be reduced to a narrowly construed rationality have been relegated to the feminine, including, as many contemporary cultural critics have noted, religion. We note an irony: While the history of education has been in one sense a history of inclusion, the stories that we have learned to tell are stories of exclusion, stories in which we learn what is irrelevant—mostly ourselves and others. The stories constituting our cultural heritage are the symbolic contract guaranteeing exile of the feminine.

What is at stake is the world and the way that we inflect ourselves toward it and toward those with whom we are in symbolic contact. This is not a matter that can be settled by either artistic rendering or scientific undertaking. Madeleine Grumet (1988) has insisted that when we teach we enact our relation to the world. But our own relation to the world is a transformation of our tracings of others (first our mothers and then our teachers) to the objects of this world. She says:

> It is impossible to think about teaching without thinking about a relation to the object to be known. It is impossible to think about the object to be known outside the human relationships that designate it as meaningful in our world. And it is impossible to think about teaching without making all these relations as well as their objects the matter of our study. (p. 17)

Grumet insists that all teaching is an act of inquiry, one best undertaken through narrative investigations. Narration permits us simultaneously to enter the world and reenact its relations and to enact a transformation of that world and those relations. Educational inquiry conceived and constructed as transforming of both productive and reproductive relations, of both foundation and profession, is a narrative praxis of the sort outlined in Chapter 3.

Feminist narratives have revealed to us the partial nature of our activity—partial in the sense of incomplete and in the sense of interested. Feminists have made morally problematic what Raymond Williams (1977) calls the selective tradition in Western culture. Feminist inquiry questions the selection of problems and the delineation of disciplinary fields, while challenging most of the assumptions guiding research. In its positive moment, feminist research forces us to see how, when intellectual work is gendered, and when women are included in our picture of reality, common sense itself becomes problematic. We are forced to wonder how "common" common sense is and to whom it is common. By showing us the ways in which our picture of reality, and hence our experience of reality, changes when the frame includes women, feminists have eroded the traditional oppositions between objectivity and subjectivity, fact and value, theory and practice, knower and known, the political and the personal, and, necessarily, the liberal and the professional. Feminist theory teaches us to tell stories, to narrate in our own voices.

EDUCATION AND HUMAN INTERESTS

Recent work in the field of curriculum and teaching, drawing on more general critiques of prevailing views of knowledge, begins with the assumption that human interest is constitutive of our paradigms of knowledge, that these interested paradigms determine appropriate objects of knowledge and define legitimate relationships between knowers and known. Critics charge that insisting on those oppositions challenged by feminist theory proceeds from an ideology in which theory serves to maintain the status quo. This ideology assimilates knowledge to commodities in such a way as to reduce all human relationships to relationships among commodities. The exchange paradigm within which classroom relations are negotiated and the ways in which classroom commodities are distributed and claimed all reproduce the dominant relations of patriarchy. The fact of representation, of the way that the curriculum represents the world and its social relations, is all-important. We are concerned not only with absence and presence, but with the very modalities of representation.

Feminists and other curriculum theorists argue that the traditional oppositions that their work exposes and disrupts hold us enthralled and enslaved by mystifying our own activity as knowers. These oppositions, in mystifying the sensual, creative nature of knowledge production and reproduction, support practices that bar access for many to the high-status knowledge necessary to achieving social and economic power. More important for feminist theorists is that they provide a foundation not just for excluding, but for denigrating, unvalued modes of knowing and experience. In the movies they call it "gaslighting." In feminist narratives it is enacted as the experience of being always wrong. In trying to free us from our enthrallment, feminist theory challenges the grammar and syntax of patriarchal knowledge, but in doing so more fully instantiates the values of liberal education.

We often feel an inclination to exclude patriarchal knowledge from the curriculum and replace it with something else. That is a mistake. It is a mistake not because patriarchal knowledge is not elitist or violent, but because its elitism and intrinsic violence are beside the point from a pedagogical point of view. The patriarchal cultural heritage both is and is not the cultural heritage of all who do not occupy its privileged spaces. It is the knowledge by which all others are defined as Other. (This is the culture whose texts enable us to feel our lives figured in those of others, to see ourselves writ large and small.) In that culture women are either absent or translated into images of primal male fantasy and anxiety. The same is true of people of color and members of the working classes. A liberal education would teach us to interrogate that culture. We can come to those texts with new eyes and ask how they function in our lives. Rather than asking what those texts give to us, what we receive from them, as we do within a patriarchal paradigm, we can shift the frame and ask what we can take from such texts. We can look for the blind spot in the dream of patriarchy and wake ourselves from that dream.

A number of psychoanalytic theorists, following the work of Jacques Lacan (1985), argue that subject–object relations, the very constitution of human subjectivity and hence the constitution of that which subjectivity intends, is rooted in a double patriarchal anxiety (Gallop, 1985; Irigaray, 1985). The first is the male's uncertainty that his wife's offspring are indeed his own. The second is the anxiety that attends the renunciation of desire for the mother demanded by the law of patriarchy. The Name-of-the-Father becomes an invocation permitting the male to make the inference of paternity, thereby ensuring the proper exchange of property. The law of patriarchy also assures the power of the exchange of women among men. The structure of language and knowledge both are permeated by uncertainty and by unconscious conflicts attending separation from the all-powerful, phallic mother. For Lacan, the subject, the speaking "I," emerges at the moment when the child recognizes the impossibility of achieving the desired primordial union with the mother and becomes aware of the father's prohibition of this desire. Fearing castration, the child rejects the mother. For Lacan, then, the unconscious is feminine, while the conscious is wholly masculine, originating as it does in the prohibition of patriarchal law. Language is the mark of difference. Knowledge is the knowledge of sexual difference. But our valorized modes of reasoning compensate for this tragedy. The superiority of inference over immediate knowledge elevates paternity over maternity. The rational modes of assimilation and analogy can be seen as attempts to deny that difference out of which consciousness is born. We search for what is like and deny that which is unlike. Civilization as we know it is the inscription of patriarchy as owner of the symbolic contract.

It may be tempting simply to reject language, to promote a cult of the unconscious, of the primal mother, the phallic mother who both nurtures and avenges. There are a couple of obstacles in the way of such a move. First, it is difficult to imagine what an escape from language would amount to: Escape to what? We find ourselves in language, albeit in the language of the fathers. A false dilemma is set up, but a dilemma that William Bennett, for example, relies on our accepting as real when he attacks the Stanford revision of core requirements (McCurdy, 1988). Either we teach the pleasures of irony or we encourage our students to wallow in sentimentality. Either we teach Henry James or we teach working-class narratives. Either we teach literature or we teach something that is not literature. In each opposition the first term is superior and threatened with disruption and effacement by the second. But no one is asking that such choices be made. The point is not to reject the rational but to appropriate it, to deflect rationality from its Enlightenment trajectory.

The second objection is that such a romantic rejection of language requires an inversion that Nel Noddings (1984) cautions against: It makes feminine nature—those capacities we have come to associate with relatedness, caring, and nurture—the *source* of female experience, rather than understanding that what we call feminine nature (and masculine nature) is the *consequence* of female experience (and male experience). Even Freud knew that, despite some lapses in memory. Noddings (1984) thinks that righting this inversion is critical, because her project is to construct a new ideal of the educated person (our liberal arts student for example)—an ideal in which we strive to develop in males as well as in females those capacities we value under the rubric "feminine." This project avoids the temptation to value one sex over the other; it urges that the masculine rational and the feminine suprarational be equally valued and mixed, in conversation, in all persons.

FEMINIST SCHOLARSHIP, EDUCATION, AND PROFESSIONALISM

Like our civilization, the education that is its handmaiden is grounded in fear and hostility. The image of the artist or genius represented in the canon is an image of separateness and specialness. Conflict between self and other, self and society defines the artist's existence. So too goes the life of genius. There is our liberal arts curriculum, the purest expression of the idea/ideal (*eidos/eidōlon*) of the university. This is a violent curriculum, one that can breed only more injury and violence or else indifference in the face of the violence that describes this thing we call "civilization." If professional preparation is an application of the knowledge produced and reproduced through this curriculum, professional practice is either indifferent or an expression of violence.

Each historical moment contains the potential for positive change. Side by side with the reform initiatives we criticize is an increase in the number and size of women's studies programs and an interest in integrating what has been learned in two decades of feminist scholarship into the liberal arts curriculum. The integration project involves considerably greater adjustments than simply choosing between Henry Adams and Charlotte Brontë or adding a woman or two to the syllabus in introductory courses. The project is one that would revolutionize our understanding of the liberal arts, and not just by exposing the way in which liberal arts study reproduces the gender and racial politics of patriarchy. This project revolutionizes our conception of the relationship between knowledge and practice and disrupts the logic of domination. This project is an expression of a radical re-visioning of educational inquiry. Educational inquiry re-visioned becomes praxis.

Feminist scholarship teaches the habits of mind and heart that Barbara Du Bois (1983) calls "passionate scholarship," habits of thinking and feeling that implicate us personally in our work and our world. To integrate women's studies is to make these habits of mind and heart the standard mode of teaching, a passionate pedagogy. To liberate the liberal arts and to humanize the professions requires us to come to them bearing those habits of mind and heart.

To begin with, a passionate pedagogy is a personal one. It demands that we look for ourselves in our engagement with texts and that we try to understand the ways in which information informs and transforms us. It demands that we reconstruct our notions of what it means to be a speaking subject. Within the patriarchal paradigm, knowledge is a cold, hard, straight, and clear thing uttered through but not by subjects: "One thinks that . . ." "It is generally believed that . . ." This is knowledge used to intimidate, to overwhelm, to dominate. The facts speak for themselves.

We are trying to construct an ideal of an educated person in which that cold, hard, straight, and clear thing called knowledge is understood as rooted in the knower's relatedness, in the knower's projection of self into the world. Our ideal of knowledge is, in fact, implied in stated goals of the liberal arts once they are scrutinized from a critical perspective. The ideal of the educated person is one in whom habits of the mind and habits of the heart are mixed in a passionate caring for the world we intend through our acts of knowing. The educated person not only possesses, he or she is, a past and a future. We find and form not only ourselves through language and knowledge. In language and knowledge we find and form our world. Only those who recognize their radical nearness to the world, their radical responsibility for that world, are liberally educated.

The business of entering a conversation is a tricky one. Women, and all other Others, find themselves on the side of the second term in our most venerable oppositions, for example, mind/body, individual/community, reason/emotion. It is far easier for women to follow their brothers into the sleep of reason or to retreat to alternating cycles of feminine silence and frenzies of prophecy. At the center of the conversation is the aim of negotiating the claims of community and the claims of the individual, the claims of reason and the claims of the emotions, the claims of the mind and the claims of the body.

A cultural heritage that transmits and invites conversation will be necessarily different from that tradition exemplified in Cardinal Newman's (1852/1976) notion of an education and of teaching. It will be different from that tradition so desperately and aggressively reconsecrated by conservative reformers.

Knowledge, liberal knowledge, the knowledge of civilization, compensates for the patriarchal anxiety it represses, and it is in its compensatory role that we may say it is a good in itself. It enables us, as Newman taught, to know the relative dispositions of things. For not to know the "relative dispositions of things is the state of slaves or children; to have mapped out the Universe is the boast of Philosophy" (p. 35). But what is repressed always returns.

Our purpose in shaping general liberal education programs is to make ourselves known to ourselves, not, as students commonly suppose, to give them culture or simply to add more requirements to their already overburdened, unfree lives. To make ourselves known to ourselves is to find out where we are by looking at where we have been; to make ourselves known to ourselves is a project in re-vision of impressions of old familiar places and faces. The goals of liberal education, educational inquiry, and feminist theory intersect just here.

Feminist theory is a theory of practice—to theorize, to see—a seeing of practice. Feminist theory is practical theory. It is theory of reading, of writing, and of teaching. In asking us to consider what it might be like to read, to write, and to teach as a woman, it asks us to undertake to find the self lost in, bewitched, and subdued by language. It asks us to undertake to find the self lost in the civilization of modernity.

In this undertaking we may reconstruct the profession of the liberal arts. In understanding who we are, men and women both, we turn to issues of gender because our experience of ourselves is fundamentally an experience of sexed beings and because our experience of the world is experience of a world ordered by gender. Because woman is, in the beginning (In the beginning was the Word—the Name-of-the-Father), excluded from language, can speak only in the words of the Father, woman's situation is a model for the situation of all, men and women alike, who are lost in language and deformed by information. This is not an essentialist position.

Within the patriarchal paradigm, knowledge, like all other goods, becomes hostile to the knowers, becomes alien, a commodity for exchange. To think, to speak, to write, to teach, to learn as a woman is first to adopt an attitude antithetical to commodity relations, an attitude of expectation, engagement, enjoyment, and surprise. This is an attitude that men as well as women can adopt. The second step requires that we attach our language to things and to particular lives (that we make the Word flesh). Men as well as women can do this. And men as well as women can undertake the sort of critical analysis of texts and language, of processes and institutions, that shows what is concealed and excluded in what is revealed and included.

The moment of surprise, the moment when we arrive at old places, encounter familiar faces, turns us from answers to questions, turns answers to questions and questions to answers. The moment of encounter that disrupts all hierarchies and oppositions turns us to professional praxis, to the public calling that is teaching. We learn that things congeal in the answer; the world begins and is passed on in the question. The answer is a commodity; the question, a gift. To participate in professional praxis, to profess, is to pass on the gift. Professional practice must be located in a gift rather than a market economy, in a logic of conversation rather than of domination. The commodity enslaves; the gift liberates.

The root sense of the word *profession* carries with it a baggage of public declaration and public commitment, a sense of calling and of witnessing. Education as a field of liberal study examines the nature of those declarations and commitments and the ways in which our experiences in and out of institutions are implicated in the development of those public declarations and commitments. Education as a field of liberal study is education for professional praxis. In the following chapter we examine both educational inquiry and the profession of teaching as these have supported and continue to maintain the ways of thinking and feeling that dominate the cultural heritage passed on through our liberal arts institutions. We explore there ways of conceiving both inquiry and practice as a synoptic field of action, the aim of which may be seen as one of recivilization.

CHAPTER 6

Ideology and the Preparation
of Schoolteachers

The general view articulated in this volume is that educational studies inquires into the ways in which society maintains itself over time and the ways of thinking and feeling that dominate as a result of that process of social reproduction. We have shown how conceptions of professionalism have fostered the process of social reproduction in a number of ways, in various social and occupational contexts. Contrary to a dominant conception of professionalism founded on technical rationality, a complete and well-understood professionalism must include as a vital element the notion of praxis, as professionals mediate and interpret the relationships between the clients and relevant professional arenas and interactions (whether this involves the courtroom, surgical procedures, or curricular materials). We have also indicated how liberal studies themselves have been involved in the social reproduction of gender relations. Through recapturing the value of difference, relatedness, and literalness, education can lead to nonpatriarchal forms of re-visioned social life.

The last few years have been interesting ones for those concerned with schooling in the United States. Numerous organizations, agencies, and individuals have analyzed current educational problems and proposed reforms to redress them (see Adler, 1982; Boyer, 1983; Goodlad, 1984; Lightfoot, 1983; National Commission on Excellence in Education, 1983; and Sizer, 1984). A variety of educational and social issues have been noted in this literature—from falling test scores and teacher disaffection to a decline in military strength and a loss of economic supremacy. These purported school failures have resulted in school reforms favoring, among other things, more stringent high school graduation requirements, increased homework assignments for students, proposals for greater supervision of prospective and professional teachers, and increased salaries for employees. This school reform literature has been accompanied by attempts to reform teacher preparation (see Carnegie Forum on Education and the Economy, 1986; Holmes Group, 1986; National Commission for Excellence in Teacher Education, 1985; Southern Regional Education Board, n.d.). In part this was due to a tendency to see teachers as central figures in school reform, so that by improving the quality of teacher preparation we might thereby enhance the quality of our public educational institutions.

If we are to understand the current efforts to reform schools and teacher-preparation programs, we must be sensitive to the array of social and historical interests out of which these reforms have grown. In particular, the effort to raise the status of the teaching profession has a rather long history in this country, one that is closely tied to the dynamics of reproduction through class and gender relations. As we saw in our previous discussions of professionalism and teaching, understanding the concepts, assumptions, and actions that dominate at a particular time requires that we place them in the context of that time.

As noted in the Introduction, a number of ideas and social currents helped shape educational thought in the United States prior to the advent of public educational institutions. A basic faith in progress and personal improvement fit nicely with the view that the people must take responsibility for governance. Democratic practices were accompanied by an emphasis on pragmatic action, sometimes at the expense of theoretical reflection and analysis. At the same time, American individualism and self-reliance undergirded our vision of social and economic progress. The recognition of social inequality, especially as this was intensified by tensions between capital and labor through the emergence of factory capitalism, made more obvious the antagonisms that threatened to undermine political and economic values. Especially as immigration increased, people with divergent ideologies and practices seemed, in the view of some, to threaten social cohesion. This conglomeration of political assumptions, religious convictions, economic realities, and moral sentiments formed the backdrop for American efforts to provide institutions of public education.

An important irony must be noted in the ways in which teacher preparation has been implicated in the process of social reproduction. From the beginning of teacher preparation as an association of people devoted to moral revival, through the development of the normal schools and subsequently the teachers colleges, educational leaders have insisted on apolitical, asocial practices in both public schools and teacher–preparation institutions. They have sought a neutral plane, a safe haven within which agreed-on principles and ideas would dominate and controversy, divisiveness, and ideology would be avoidable. Yet in the process teachers and those responsible for their preparation have enveloped schools within prevailing political, economic, and ideological forces.

In the end, the search for neutrality has linked schools and teachers even more tightly to prevailing social patterns. The process of social reproduction is thereby made more compelling, as schoolpeople offer the appearance of noninvolvement in social and political affairs at the same time that their values and directions link school practice to accepted patterns. This is apparent, as noted in the Introduction to this volume, in the desire of spokespersons for public schools and teacher–training institutions to avoid controversy within educational practice. Conflict was avoided by

1. Fashioning a proper American character through common schooling
2. Training normal school graduates who would reflect the expressed wishes of the community, matching their concerns to the interests of the community
3. Teachers voicing an impatience with discussing educational ideas and values, wanting instead to learn about teaching techniques and strategies
4. Separating academic study and professional preparation
5. Divorcing action from reflection

In fostering accommodation to accepted practices, apolitical posturing, gender-specific social and economic relations, and an at least implicit acceptance of the educational and social status quo, teacher–preparation programs have contributed to social and ideological continuity. Here we see how the common sense of educational practice, an understandable desire to fit into patterns of American social life and be accepted as a worthy profession, actually furthered the process of unequal social reproduction. Normal school advocates separated their endeavors from the colleges and universities, taking a largely vocational/technical training cue from common school practices as these had been defined *for* them. In taking a noncritical, unproblematic view of schoolkeeping; accepting the class and gender variables of education as natural or normal; and seeking to promote a particular vision of moral propriety that would outlaw contentious ideas and promote an economically useful hidden curriculum, programs of teacher preparation have historically promoted the uncritical continuation of educational and social practices.

Commenting on trends in teacher education (in both normal schools and teachers colleges) from the 1890s through the early 1950s, Harold Rugg (1952) expresses a number of ideas that summarize the dominant political orientation surrounding teacher preparation in the United States:

> One who visits the universities and liberal arts colleges today senses a widespread inertia among those who are training our teachers. This inertia should really cause little wonder. It is the product of recognizable forces in the culture and the perpetuation of the basic pattern that has been fastened on teacher education for fifty years. The forces surrounding the teachers have conspired to make them timid about making over the schools, or the teacher–education program. The communities in which they went to school and the climate of opinion in their colleges warned them not to be too active. The standard pattern of teacher education taught that the school was to pass *on* the social heritage; it was not to appraise the social order, let alone try to change it. Teachers were to fit into the society. . . . They were practical men. (p. 22)

Nor is this an exclusively historical tendency. Many contemporary teacher–preparation programs have reflected a similar perspective on current patterns in schools and the wider society. The dominant rationality in teacher–preparation programs continues to be technical and pragmatic, removing teacher preparation from larger social, political, and moral debates.[1] This rationality is perhaps most explicit in contemporary proposals for

---

[1]Some of the ideas outlined in this section were published in a preliminary version in Beyer and Zeichner, 1987.

competency-based teacher preparation, the competency testing of teachers, apprenticeship-oriented clinical teacher training, systems management approaches to curriculum development and program evaluation, behaviorist psychologies, and state licensing requirements. To take but one example, advocates of "research-based teacher education"—a recent euphemism for competency-based teacher training—strive to develop specific teaching skills or strategies in isolation from both the curricular context within which such skills are to be developed and larger debates about the social and political aims toward which they are directed. For instance, much attention has been paid of late to the importance of teachers' asking "higher-order questions." Yet the specific context of a classroom—the lack of autonomy for teachers and the tendency for tedium to replace inquiry—directly affects the possibility that such higher-order questions might actually be asked and inhibits the transformation that can occur in the process of asking them. The possible value of higher-order questions about literature in an elementary school classroom, for example, needs to be seen in light of the forms of pedagogy associated with a basal reading series (Shannon, 1989).

Again, current discussions surrounding "cooperative learning" can devolve into another series of abstract debates about "proper instructional methods." Such discussions are, in fact, likely to become isolated in this way, given the technical/pragmatic, patriarchal rationality that dominates in teacher training. To prevent this isolation, such issues must be integrated with questions about the proper aims of education and their relationship to essentially moral questions about the desirability of social reproduction or transformation (Wood, 1984). Like the efforts of historic school reformers, the current emphasis on technical rationality has led to a trivialization of the relationships between teacher and learner by assigning to teachers the role of a technical, value-free manager of activities over which they have little or no control. The moral and social issues embedded in the processes of the classroom are obscured as teacher trainers focus attention on procedures to attain ends that are not openly examined.

The current reform movement in teacher preparation has also largely replicated historic tendencies in the field. In particular, the split between academic and professional studies seen in the separation of normal schools from other institutions of higher education is reinforced in much of the reform literature. For example, the Carnegie Forum on Education and the Economy

(1986) says that "the undergraduate years should be wholly devoted to a broad liberal education and a thorough grounding in
the subjects to be taught. The professional education of teachers
should therefore take place at the graduate level" (p. 73). Likewise, the Holmes Group (1986) says that education cannot be a
proper subject-area major at the undergraduate level. Instead,
"academic" courses of study, which will provide the necessary
grounding for professional education, must be emphasized. Professional preparation will then be concerned with the translation
of academic content into effective teaching strategies through an
affiliation with the behavioral sciences. Such separation of education from other fields of study would continue the historic separation of professional education—largely on the Parsonian model
of the professions discussed in chapter 3—from academic inquiry
that dominated the history of normal school training.

Yet other possibilities for the development of teacher preparation have been attempted, such as the American Institute of
Instruction mentioned in the Introduction. And contemporary
alternatives are being promoted as well. The remainder of this
chapter will highlight such an alternative direction. The central
aim of the alternative we support is to emphasize the essentially
political nature of education—the very thing that normal school
advocates and contemporary spokespersons for the reform of
teacher preparation have either ignored or sought to hide.

TEACHER PREPARATION, PRAXIS, AND ALTERNATIVE SOCIAL REALITIES

Our orientation to teacher preparation denies the split
between academic and applied study, liberal and professional
endeavors, that has become commonsensical in American educational thought. Our approach to the preparation of schoolteachers avoids the dangers of an aloof scholasticism on the one
hand and a technical/pragmatic rationality on the other (see
Beyer, 1988b).

One of our central claims is that educational studies is a part
of reconstituted liberal learning that binds together reason and
emotion, thought and action. Given the history of education and
of teacher training in the United States, this is neither an obvious
conclusion nor one reflected in educational practices in schools
and colleges offering professional courses for teachers.

Educational studies as a domain of inquiry is essentially integrative or synoptic in orientation. It seeks to synthesize a variety of
methodologies, issues, and areas of research, integrating perspectives and issues from a number of areas without being reduced to
any of them in isolation. The synthetic nature of education as a
field of inquiry is due in part to the multidimensionality of what it
means, or can mean, to be an educated woman or man. While there
are particular purposes that schools and colleges can further, none
of these captures the general meaning of "becoming educated." In
Democracy and Education, Dewey (1916) wrote:

> With the renewal of physical existence goes, in the case of
> human beings, the re-creation of beliefs, ideals, hopes, happi-
> ness, misery, and practices. The continuity of any experience,
> through renewing of the social group, is a literal fact. Educa-
> tion, in its broadest sense, is the means of this social continuity
> of life. (p. 2)

In providing for such continuity, education must be understood
as including virtually all aspects of individual and social life, as we
consider the wealth of experiences of which people are capable.
Moreover, the study of education must consider "continuity" in
its broadest social sense: not only as understanding and reinforcing current practices but also as making possible and accessible
alternative ones through the construction of educative possibilities. To engage in educational studies is to consider the full range
of interactions, meanings, ideas, and values to which people do or
can give voice.

Conceived in this admittedly overarching way, it is clear that
educational studies requires a wide range of investigations and
inquiries. A recognition of the complexities involved in education
has given rise to the need for an expanded set of tools with which
to understand the dynamics of education. Recent studies have
highlighted the importance of ethnographic, qualitative, and participant studies, which add a needed dimension to our empirical
accounts of what it means to educate and be educated. The
insights made available through historical, philosophical, and sociological studies of education have also proven to be of major
importance. Further, the work of scholars in women's studies,
black studies, cultural studies, and other more critically oriented
traditions—as outlined in previous chapters—has been crucial in
helping us see and come to grips with the dynamics of educative

and miseducative experience. These traditions are synthesized in educational studies in a way that differentiates them from other, more traditional areas of liberal learning that have tended to become specialized and even fragmented.

The integrative strength of educational studies is of special importance for the preparation of schoolteachers, conceived as a part of such study. The moral responsibility of educated women and men, the nature of knowledge and its transmission to others, the relationship between social justice, individual lives, the family, and other institutions and practices, the appropriate values for a democratic state, and so on—all these require careful scrutiny by all of us. They are especially important issues for those who would educate our children. As such, those involved in teacher preparation must recognize their comprehensive responsibilities:

> Many students of teacher education have stressed the fact that more than technical or applicative knowledge is involved in the effort to function as a professional. They have stressed the importance of inquiry into the "interpretive context," meaning the ideational and socio-cultural contexts of teaching and learning as they proceed in schools. . . . They have stressed the fact that teachers are not only obliged to become scholars and theorists in specialized fields but persons explicitly concerned with the polity and the kinds of action that make a difference in the public space. (Greene, 1978, p. 59)

Here we choose to affiliate with at least a portion of the legacy of teacher preparation. We conceive of education and teaching as essentially moral phenomena, built on practical wisdom rather than technocratic rationality. We also agree with Beecher's claim that the central commitment of teachers must be "to do good." Yet unlike the historical figures involved in reform, and many contemporary advocates as well, we acknowledge the political, economic, and social dimensions of the moral responsibility of teachers. Because we are teachers and because we acknowledge the political nature of all teaching, our moral sensibilities are informed by the political dimensions of our actions. Moreover, again unlike both historical and contemporary advocates of reform, we promote an alternative conception of educational studies that rehabilitates liberal learning while promoting a more contextualized picture of educational inquiry. Teachers, most of whom are women, must not be regarded as technicians pursuing taken-for-granted ends defined by others; nor should their education proceed as a kind of vocational training.

More than anything else, public school teachers must be able to exercise judgment, to think critically and reflectively about the nature and conditions of their work, to continue intellectual engagement with others as a part of their professional identity, and to deal with the complexities of an environment that frequently places a number of stresses on their time and energy—stresses that are due in no small measure to the political and ideological cross-currents in which, as we have seen, schools are placed. Teachers need the very orientations and habits of heart and mind that are prized by spokespersons for the liberal arts.

Yet educational studies integrates areas that go beyond liberal learning as often understood, highlighting the importance of action as well as thought, feeling as well as thinking, doing as well as analyzing. Many writers have claimed that liberal learning improves "the life of the mind," increases tolerance, engenders a love of learning outside formal institutions, and generally helps to civilize human life. What educational studies provides is the critically important function of questioning whether "the life of the mind" should or can be adequately conceived apart from the pursuit of personal well-being and social justice. Concerned with political ideas and moral principles, educational studies is equally committed to ethical conduct; committed to social justice, it seeks avenues for its concrete expression in practice; impressed with the need for reason, care, and reflection, it promotes practical actions that embody these qualities in a human context. Educational inquiry not only respects liberal learning; it also articulates ways to further such learning in the real, social, interactive contexts in which people live. It seeks to bridge the chasm between theory and practice that has been built into so many institutions of higher education and that is reinforced in both the history of teacher preparation and the current call for its reform. The peculiar power of educational studies is its commitment to personal and social praxis; its ability to enlarge the mind in ways that connect it to the body, to practical action, and to the social good. As a field of moral action, educational studies has much to offer students regardless of academic major or projected occupation. It also promises a reconceptualized program of teacher preparation.

TEACHER EDUCATION AS PRAXIS

While the historical and contemporary trends in teacher preparation have provided powerful precedents, they have by no means been all-encompassing. The possibility that programs for the preparation of schoolteachers might be altered so as to consciously reorient patterns of social reproduction has often been discussed, and some strategies for developing program directions along these lines have been presented (see, e.g., Barone, 1987; Beyer, 1984; Beyer & Zeichner, 1987; Goodman, 1986; Liston & Zeichner, 1987; Zeichner, 1980). Such efforts have done much to uncover the short- and long-term consequences of teacher preparation, just as they have illuminated its theoretical and practical reconceptualization. The remainder of this chapter will discuss two specific attempts to put into practice such a conception of teacher preparation[2] (see also Beyer, 1989; Laird, 1988).

Case Study A

The setting for this alternative model for teacher preparation was a small, church-related, liberal arts college in the rural Midwest. Faculty, administrators, and students saw the college as a teaching institution, with little or no expectation for faculty research projects. Like other schools of its type and size, frequent and prolonged faculty–student relationships were advocated and expected. This tendency was exaggerated by the adoption during the late 1970s of a rather unique calendar, for which the college attained some notoriety in the national press. Faculty members taught, and students were enrolled in, one course for each of the nine "blocks," each lasting three and one-half weeks, that constituted the academic year. This ensured that faculty and students—who often met in classes lasting three or more hours each day—would have in-depth, frequent contact.

Founded in the 1850s, the college had a long history of providing programs for those students interested in pursuing teaching as a possible career. In the recent past, before the initiation of alternative programs, the institution had become increas-

---

[2]The case studies presented in this chapter are based on the professional experiences of two of the authors.

ingly concerned about (1) the isolation of the department of education from the rest of the college (accompanied by a vague uneasiness that its programs were not as demanding as those in other departments) and (2) the possibility that, given the current national climate for the reform of teacher education, undergraduate teacher-preparation programs might be eliminated in the near future.

In response to the latter possibility, the consortium of institutions of higher education of which the college was a member had held a special conference to consider the role of departments of education within the liberal arts. This conference sparked a good deal of campus debate, both about the quality and nature of current teacher-preparation programs as well as possible alternatives. When both previous members of the department of education retired in the years 1985–1987, the college found itself in a position to hire faculty members who might reinvigorate teacher preparation on campus by outlining directions that had not been pursued by former members of the faculty.

As a result, teacher-preparation program proposals were created that were consistent with the depiction of educational studies discussed in this and previous chapters. The programs developed at this college

1. Raised as central themes the dynamics of social inequality (by gender, social class, ethnicity, race, and age) and their implications for schooling and teaching
2. Incorporated a critical perspective into coursework and practical experiences in the schools so that classroom interventions became opportunities for political and ethical action
3. Emphasized the responsibility of teachers in the creation, implementation, and evaluation of curricula and pedagogy that are intertwined with the dynamics of reproduction
4. Stressed the need for students to avoid uncritical acceptance of the ideas, claims, and interests of others, and instead to actively pursue their own education, emphasizing the development of meaning in their own contexts
5. Focused on the importance of developing philosophical approaches to teaching and curriculum with which more concrete pedagogical and curricular activities could be undertaken in schools

6. Emphasized a view of schools and teaching as embedded within social parameters that often had been largely obscured through a reliance on behaviorist psychology and objectivist epistemologies that are seriously flawed (Beyer, 1988a)
7. Fostered a consideration of the idea that the current world of schooling is only one among several possibilities, favoring the interests of some groups more than others

Such efforts reflected the trust that students can become autonomous, morally engaged, reflective teachers who take and argue for positions and actions that are well formulated and yet responsive to those whose ideas diverge from their own.

Within this alternative, it was recommended that the name of the department be changed to "Educational Studies" and that students be allowed to obtain a major in the department by (1) completing a program of study that combined education with other courses in a way that reflects our view that educational studies embody an integrated frame of reference; such a major would not lead to certification; or (2) completing a program that would lead to elementary or secondary certification.

Consistent with the view that education is an integrative area of inquiry not limited to the training of future teachers, interdisciplinary and team-taught courses were proposed as viable possibilities. In addition, it was suggested that courses in the foundations of education be cross-listed within departments of history, philosophy, psychology, and sociology and receive distribution credit in the appropriate division of the college.

The specific proposal for teacher preparation, reflecting the view of educational studies discussed in this book, included the following courses, leading to a teaching certificate in elementary education:

1. Educational Psychology
2. History of U.S. Education
3. Educational Philosophies or Educational Philosophies, Fiction, and Gender
4. Schooling in American Society
5. Processes of Educational Labeling and the Politics of Difference
6. Curriculum, Pedagogy, and Ideology

7. Aesthetics and the Culture of Schooling
8. Epistemology and the Predicaments of Schooling
9. Educational Praxis
10. Student Teaching (2 courses)
11. Senior Thesis

The new program in elementary education consisted of four more or less traditional foundations courses (in the psychology, history, philosophy, and sociology of education—course numbers 1, 2, 3, and 4, above), with some important differences. While these courses were to provide the conceptual and analytic tools with which to engage in the more concrete work of curriculum development and pedagogical experimentation that followed, the perspectives embodied in these courses were incorporated into subsequent ones (numbers 5 through 11, above); just as school-based experiences that were included in the latter courses employed the analytic and interpretive inclinations of the foundations sequence.

The first series of courses would provide students with the necessary critical and interpretive understandings for the work of teaching conceived as praxis. The latter courses in the program would be committed to the integration of theoretical understanding and practical action, as students created, implemented, and reflected upon curriculum projects and teaching activities in local schools. Consistent with a prominent theme of this volume, there would be no sharp break between any of the courses in the program, with each emphasizing the competence needed for critical understanding that would lead to practical action by professionals.

Programs of teacher preparation based on such ideas and curricular proposals are likely to encounter resistance at many institutions. Again, an actual set of experiences along this line may be helpful in assessing the possibilities for alternatives in teacher preparation that highlight the political, moral, and educational—as opposed to merely training, normal school–oriented—nature of teacher preparation.

The reasons for the eventual dilution of the recommendations for educational studies and programs of teacher preparation summarized above are closely tied to larger institutional and ideological contexts. Running through some of the criticisms of these program proposals was, at one level, the issue of "turf": what courses should be offered in what department, by which instructor (this was an especially pointed question with respect to the course in philosophy of education). The usual concerns were voiced about expertise, appropriate background, availability of staff, and the like—more or less empirical questions that could, one supposes, be resolved by examining the evidence. Yet at another level the issue of "turf" was only a cover for another, more deeply felt concern. While discussions of program proposals in terms of their political sentiments were purposely avoided, the traditional view of the liberal arts as concerned with "pure knowledge," "dispassionate inquiry," and "the search for truth" was being challenged. It was argued, instead, that what counts as knowledge—indeed as education itself—cannot be separated from the larger social, political, and ideological contexts out of which claims to knowledge arise and are debated.

Of course debating the epistemological issues involved in this dispute might well be seen as itself part of liberal inquiry (see, e.g., Graff, 1987). Yet it is quite rare for faculty in departments of education to be seen as central figures in such debates—a predicament that reflects the traditionally low status of education in colleges and universities. In the case under examination here, the closest the faculty came to a discussion of such important issues was a question about the use of "ideology" in the title of the course that dealt with curriculum and pedagogy. Similar questions were raised about the use of "aesthetics" and "epistemology" in other recommended course titles. Thus what looked like a complicated and interesting philosophical issue that has implications for virtually all areas of the college curriculum never really surfaced; it was replaced by technical/procedural questions that kept hidden the very kinds of issues liberal inquiry is alleged to help resolve.

More expansively, there was a tendency for "liberal/technical proceduralism" to supplant more substantive, informed intellectual engagement. Questions raised during committee deliberations were often technical in nature (what new course will count for which old one, what response might there be from the state department of education regarding certification requirements, how does the total number of courses compare with requirements for other majors) or peripheral, as discussed in the preceding paragraph.

Faculty members asked questions about how these curricular reform proposals differed from those offered by other institutions with which comparisons were often made. A few members of the faculty requested the names of institutions that had implemented similar programs or were contemplating doing so. While such questions may arise when any program is being substantially overhauled, in the case of education programs these questions may be more often repeated, and asked with more intensity, than might be true for other departments. There is frequently a reluctance for faculty and administrators to be seen as promoting an educational program that is out of the ordinary. Such a conservative intellectual posture, when accompanied by liberal proceduralism, was effective in undermining, though not challenging, our proposals. Within such an environment, a rather small group of faculty members functioned so as to subvert proposals it saw as objectionable (for psychological as well as political reasons), without benefit of intellectual engagement with the ideas involved and even without benefit of public debate.

An especially disturbing tendency in at least some institutions of higher education needs to be noted here as well. Especially in private institutions, where tuition payments represent a substantial proportion of the college's income, there is a growing tendency to substitute market values for intellectual commitments. Faculty in the case being discussed here were exhorted to identify students who might transfer to other institutions so that they might be encouraged not to do so. Even more revealing was the decision, mentioned earlier, to implement a rather novel calendar. The rather overt purpose in adopting this calendar was to increase enrollments. Yet the possible intellectual and pedagogical consequences of that decision were not fully discussed or debated. Administrators also made reference, from time to time, to helping faculty "graduate a better product." Both faculty and administration were genuinely pleased when a popular financial magazine listed the college as one of the "10 best buys" in higher education, missing the ambiguity in this message. The nature of "caring" needs careful analysis in an institution where market and academic values become conflated. In substituting market values for intellectual engagement and debate, and combining this with the technical/liberal proceduralism and intellectual conservatism already noted, the culture of this college exhibited little respect for the very traditions of inquiry it allegedly embodied.

When this happens, proposals for the reform of teacher preparation based on our conception of educational studies are likely to arouse concern not over what is intellectually or pedagogically appropriate or how expected anxiety about curricular changes can be engaged and resolved in an educative way. Rather, a primary concern is likely to be what the material consequences of student anxiety might be.

What can we learn from the attempts to introduce an alternative conception of teacher preparation as praxis at this institution, and the resistance it encountered?

First, while faculty members had doubts about the efficacy of previous teacher-preparation courses and programs, many saw these as a haven for students who might not survive intellectually in other courses of study. Departments of education serve, in this way, an important institutional/economic function in providing a home for certain students. Given the dominance of market values, such hypocrisy seemed to escape notice.

Second, the politically and intellectually conservative nature of this college, as reflected in its organizational and bureaucratic structures, made such proposals suspect. Some faculty members saw such redirections as encroaching on domains that were more properly their own. This is always a danger in a multidimensional, integrative field such as educational studies.

Third, there was a reluctance to address the conceptual orientation of the proposals. This may seem perplexing, since issues of crucial importance to liberal inquiry and teaching are involved in such proposals. The traditional "weak sibling" role of education departments clearly worked against their full consideration; in part this was fostered by a culture that did not recognize the importance of intellectual conflict and commitment, especially beyond the boundaries of isolated departments. The response of this college was also related to its separation of teaching from research, with the latter receiving little if any institutional support.

Fourth, the liberal/technical proceduralism exhibited in committee structures and patterns was used to fill the vacuum left by the absence of substantive intellectual engagement. Questions of strategy, of the number of recommended new courses, of the distance proposals were from the norm, and of the possible response to reforms from the state department of education supplanted more searching debate. When such questions became substitutes for dialogue around more pressing concerns, the educative impact of dialogical understanding was thwarted. Liberal proceduralism became, in effect, a form of filibuster that undercut transformative possibilities.

Case Study B

The recent history of the education department of our second example has been rather different from the one sketched above. The education department in this second case had become an empire. The department had grown with an M.A.T. program instituted during the 1960s. Around the university, it was assumed that the education department was simply a diploma mill for M.A.T. students. Colleagues in other departments were regularly surprised to learn that members of the department of education did things in addition to teacher preparation. It was a large program whose graduates were eligible for certification at the secondary level in English, social studies, math, science, and Romance languages. A semester-long paid internship was the major attraction for students, most of whom were not those liberal arts graduates for whom the program was initially designed. Many of the students had completed undergraduate teacher-preparation programs, and the M.A.T. program seemed to them a good way to earn an income while qualifying for permanent teacher certification. At the same time, a large number of undergraduates completed the five education courses required for eligibility for temporary certification. One of these courses was a month-long student teaching experience.

The department subsequently underwent an external review of its programs. The result of that review was the toppling of an empire. The teaching staff was reduced from nine to five and three of those were initially nontenurable. The secretarial staff of five was reduced to two. Typewriters were removed from faculty offices; they did permit the department to keep the photocopy machine, however. Once the dead had been as decently buried as possible, the survivors began to construct a program, which is the one in existence at the present moment.

The teacher-preparation program is the smallest in this department. Students may enroll in it for certification at the elementary level or at the secondary level in math, science, English, and social studies. A total of 16 M.A.T. and undergraduate students will student teach this year, the largest number to do so since the program was reconstructed. The elementary education program is only in its second year and prepares teachers only at the undergraduate level.

In addition to a program of teacher education, the department also offers an education major, which is in its fourth year.

Currently 37 students have declared education as a major, and a number of others have declared it as a minor. Students who major in education are eligible to enroll in the teacher-preparation program at the elementary level but not at the secondary level. The latter are required to major in the field in which they seek certification.

While the programs are conceptually distinct, students in all of them take the same courses, with the exceptions of student teaching and courses in specific subject matter, and, for potential elementary teachers, two courses in the teaching of reading. All students are required to take a course titled "The American School," which involves a critical examination of contemporary reform proposals. Students are required to read *A Nation at Risk* and *The Paideia Proposal,* among other works, and are expected to understand the historical and philosophical dimensions of such works. Students in all programs then choose among the following courses:

> Structural Models in Education
> Basic Issues in Education
> The Politics of Education
> Race and Education
> Philosophy of Education
> Women and Education
> Child and Adolescent Development
> Childhood Education
> Education in China and Japan
> Quantitative Methods in the Social Sciences
> Qualitative Methods in the Social Sciences
> Seminar in Moral Development
> Seminar in Comparative Education

The emphasis in all of these courses is on students' developing a critical perspective and on their coming to understand their own involvement in the educational systems and institutions in which they find themselves. Whether they are education majors and/or teacher-preparation students, all are expected by the time of program completion to have engaged in critical research on contemporary educational problems, to have demonstrated an understanding of the ways in which our beliefs about education and the arrangements we make are conditioned by social and historical circumstances and by human interest, and to have understood themselves as part of the educational process. This is true of the psychologically and philosophically oriented courses and the methods courses as well as those having a more obvious social and political content. These courses are not all offered each year. There are currently six department members, five tenured or tenurable and the sixth a regular replacement for leaves and sabbaticals. Three department members are women, one is a Japanese-American male, and all are committed to the vision of education and the liberal arts set forth in this book. In addition to departmental commitments, two members participate in the women's studies program and one in Asian studies; all participate in at least one course in the general education program.

Education at this institution is no longer a haven for the helpless. Departmental courses are understood to be difficult and time-consuming; they are also very popular among students. With the exception of seminars, course enrollments run between 30 and 40 students per class. While the bad aroma associated with education departments lingers in the minds of some students and faculty, the department is, on the whole, viewed favorably. There are a number of possible reasons for what would appear to be this unique situation, having to do with unique aspects of the university.

In the first place, the university is extremely small, with only 2,600 students and just over 200 full- and part-time faculty members. Since it is located in a relatively isolated town of 3,000, 40 miles from the nearest city, the faculty all know one another and spend a good deal of time together, both socially and professionally. Faculty take very seriously their governance responsibilities, and because of the size of the university, committee work brings together people from all departments and all divisions. Departments are organized under one of three divisions—natural sciences, social sciences, and humanities. A fourth division, university studies, houses area programs such as peace studies, women's studies, Africana-Hispanic studies, international relations, Asian studies, and general education.

Although the education department is in the social sciences division, the university studies division has been extremely important in its development. All of the programs grouped together there are interdisciplinary, as are many of the courses in the education department. Working with members of other departments in those programs has contributed positively not only to the intellectual reputation of the department but also to curriculum developments within the department. As the education faculty undertake ways to connect the variety of programs in the university, they have naturally rethought and revised many of their own courses. In this connection, general education has been an important site for the development of the education department. This core program, which is required of all students, is special in its attention to diversity and contemporary life in addition to more mainstream concerns with the cultural heritage. In fact, the general education program is unique in including among its requirements work that leads students to interrogate and criticize the cultural heritage.

The general education program consists of a sequence of four courses. The first two are required of all students: "Biblical and Classical Roots of Civilization" and "The Modern Experience in the West." The latter focuses on a moment in the nineteenth century, 1850 give or take a decade. Students read novels, scientific and philosophical works, poems and autobiographical works. There is an attempt to include the seldom-heard voices of women, members of the working classes, and American slaves. Both courses attempt to enlarge students' conception of textuality by including attention to architecture, technological works, opera, plays, paintings, and sculpture.

For their third course, students choose among a number of options, all of which are investigations of non-Western cultures. Unlike the first two courses, these are not necessarily interdisciplinary in approach, since each is developed by a single instructor out of his or her own research specialty.

The fourth course returns to an interdisciplinary approach but again offers students some choice. All of these courses concern some issue in contemporary American society. Courses include "World Food and Hunger," "Cancer," "Interdisciplinary Perspectives on Women," "The Faust Myth," "Nuclear Power," and "Mass Media, Mass Society, and the Individual." These courses are team-taught by, preferably three, colleagues in different disciplines. Some combinations are geography, philosophy, and biology; English, history, and education; sociology and biology; music, history, and German; art, political science, and education. All three colleagues are present for every class meeting. The pedagogical model mixes some specialty lectures with discussion formats.

Teaching at all four levels of the sequence flows out of the classroom into the other places that students live. There are regularly scheduled evening lectures, readings, films, and musical and other performances. Some courses are taught in a special dormitory focused on general education. An off-campus semester is available to students who want to continue to explore questions raised in the course on the modern experience. Faculty teaching these courses meet regularly for self-education through readings and lectures. Those involved in the first course in the sequence have visited and studied Chartres Cathedral; those in the second studied industrial archeology in Manchester and London. A variety of grants have been made available to faculty for study and course development. Recently faculty teaching in all of the four courses met for a two-day seminar organized around the concept of space. The program models the sort of commitment to a liberal education addressed in Chapter 5. Students are not the only ones to learn from it. Many of those teaching in the program have come to question the disciplinary boundaries that keep departments separate, to interrogate the cultural heritage that would seem to go without saying, and to question the educational value of traditional lecture-mode/examination pedagogy. Pedagogy is, in fact, a topic of many staff meetings. These are, obviously, questions on which members of the education department have expended a great deal of thought. And not least important, faculty have become more collegial. It would be difficult to share a classroom with someone and not develop a serious relationship with that person. General education attempts to undo precisely those oppositions that shore up the logic of domination. Explicitly addressed are questions of theory and practice, reason and emotion, male and female, art and science, and self and other. All of the cultural myths that express these oppositions are studied and questioned.

"The Modern Experience" has been important in the evolution of the introductory education course, "The American School." In this course education faculty often make concrete connections to "The Modern Experience," since they assume that students' understanding of contemporary educational problems requires an investigation of the nineteenth century. As a result of participation in both general education and other area studies programs, members of the education department have revised a number of other departmental courses. Four years ago, "The American School" totally neglected questions of gender and race. "Race and Education" is a new course this year. Moreover, because education faculty all teach in other programs in the university and meet students in those places, students are attracted to education courses who would not otherwise have thought to enroll. The education department, as is true of all other departments, fills new positions with an eye to bringing in colleagues who will contribute to both general education and to area studies. Three people who bring with them such capacity have been hired in the past three years. Such interdisciplinary work has accomplished three things for the education department. It has resulted in an improved curriculum; it has drawn to the department a population of students not usually enrolled in education departments; it has given education faculty an opportunity to become known to colleagues elsewhere in the university.

As a result, the education department has been encouraged to experiment and to institute new programs. Eight years ago the existence of the department was in serious jeopardy. That is not true today, although there are still those on the faculty who continue to believe that education is a service department or an anomalous vocational arm.

The general situation that we have described here is crucial to teacher education as we conceive it. At this institution, some of the students who are attracted to the education department, after having had another sort of course with an education faculty member, become interested, much to their surprise and often to their parents' dismay, in teacher preparation. Rather than being motivated by pervasive vocationalism, many students develop an interest in teaching that emerges from the critical dimensions of their work in education department courses. Except for the curriculum seminar attached to the student teaching experience, future teachers are enrolled in education classes that include people bound for professional and graduate education, careers in the arts, or even corporate careers. This mix of students maintains a complexity and depth of discourse that might be endangered if all were engaged in a common enterprise. At the same time all are engaged in a common enterprise. Because of the diversity of students in the courses as well as because of the intellectual and political commitments of department members, central to both pedagogy and content is the students' own educational experiences. These form the subtext of each course and are explicitly employed in the framing of discussion. For student teachers, critical analysis of personal experience in terms of general frameworks of education and as a critique of ideology is grounded in discussions of their own classroom praxis. From the point of view of students, faculty colleagues, and cooperating teachers, teacher education appears to be successful. The reasons for this success are to be found in an analysis of the structure of the university and the relationships among colleagues possible within that structure; a departmental structure that ensures student diversity (or as much diversity as possible in an institution whose students are primarily white and upper middle class); and the location of the university in an isolated rural community.

If we compare the two situations described in this chapter, we are struck by the importance of the following. First, the existence of general education and area studies programs at the second institution, and participation in them by education department faculty, draws a more diverse population of students than those perceived to be populating education courses at the first institution. While in the first example, the persistence of legend drew to the department the sort of vocationally oriented student commonly thought to major in education or to prepare to teach, these are not the majority of students in courses offered at the second institution. A number of traditionally high-achieving students speak well of education courses and pronounce them difficult. (The most recalcitrant myth in education must be the one that equates good with difficult.) Second, the interdisciplinary ethos has resulted in a climate wherein education department members are encouraged to talk about their work and to work with members of other departments. In short, the culture of the university supports the sort of liberal arts teacher education program that exists in this institutional setting.

The cultures of the two institutions outlined in these case studies clearly had an impact on their departments of education and on the possibility of instituting reforms along the lines advocated in this chapter. Such responses to redefined programs of teacher preparation illustrate the importance of local contexts in the process of creating alternatives. Perhaps the ultimate irony is that the existence of different cultural values and ideologies within these institutions document the importance of the epistemological and political ideas we are promoting: the linkages between the dynamics of education and larger patterns of social reproduction.

CONCLUSIONS

It has become a cliché to say that ignorance of the past condemns us to its repetition. A belief in the perfectibility of humankind through reconstructed social institutions; a commitment to at least the rhetoric of democracy and civic participation; a self-reliant, individualistic pragmatism; a proliferation of social inequality promoted by capitalism; and a gender-specific view of nurturance all came to be intimated within systems of schooling and teacher education in the United States. The net effect of these tendencies was to perceive the preparation of schoolteachers in largely technical and pragmatic terms, as an example of ideologically neutral professional preparation committed to the avoidance of conflict and the procurement of social cohesion. Programs of teacher preparation promoted social reproduction through social-class, racial/ethnic and gender dynamics that had their origins in the larger society and through attitudes, dispositions, and values that isolated the school from issues of social justice and political appropriateness. The tendency to regard the preparation of teachers as *training* rather than *education* reflects the view that teachers are only technicians or managers rather than morally engaged people who must be conscious of the political consequences of educational choices.

Just as this history cannot be ignored, neither should it be dismissed in a wholesale way as hopelessly reactionary and as *only* reinforcing the status quo. We have seen how alternative possibilities have been a part of this history and the extent to which some conception of moral commitment and nurturance have been involved in definitions of teaching and teacher preparation. We have also noted the contradictory nature of the social-class and gender dynamics that are involved in men's and women's opportunities for higher education and their prospects for employment as teachers. There is much here that can profitably be reclaimed through educational studies that promote more politically sensitive programs of teacher preparation. In particular, the notion that some form of nurturance is essential for teaching is a provocative one, if it does not become mired in the dualisms of reason and emotion, head and heart (Laird, 1987). The necessity of moral commitments in teaching and the desire to do good are also crucial aspects of reconceptualized programs of teacher preparation, especially when enlivened with the political and ideological issues that accompany teaching. And the traditions of democratic participation are being rekindled in many contemporary settings and proposals (see, e.g., Bastian, Fruchter, Gittell, Greer, & Haskins, 1986; Beyer & Apple, 1988). Resolving the social and educational tensions between self-reliance and public solidarity, democratically participatory and economically exclusionary practices, is aided by an awareness of how these tensions have developed historically and how various groups have sought to resolve them.

Our discussion of the reaction to redefined programs of educational studies should make us more aware of the problems attendant upon their enactment as well. Because of the multidimensionality of educational studies, and the ideological character of teaching and teacher preparation, resistance to educational studies as a field of moral action will take both intellectual and political forms. Yet such resistance gives voice to precisely the issues we are raising in this volume: the ineradicability of political discourse as a key element of educational practice and reform. In settings where such discourse is respected and valued—where educational studies are seen as important, even vital, aspects of liberal learning—the preparation of teachers may yet become a force for the sort of transformation that can lead to a better world. The profession of teaching might then become something more than what it has been.

References

Adler, M. J. (1982). *The paideia proposal: An educational manifesto.* New York: Macmillan.

American Normal School and National Teachers' Associations. (1871). *Addresses and journal of proceedings.* Washington, DC: James H. Holmes.

Arnold, M. (1932). *Culture and anarchy.* Cambridge: Cambridge University Press. (Original work published 1869).

Barone, T. E. (1987). Educational platforms, teacher selection, and school reform: Issues emanating from a biographical case study. *Journal of Teacher Education, 38* (2), 12–17.

Bastian, A., Fruchter, N., Gittell, M., Greer, C., & Haskins, K. (1986). *Choosing equality: The case for democratic schooling.* Philadelphia: Temple University Press.

Bayles, M. D. (1981). *Professional ethics.* Belmont, CA: Wadsworth.

Beiner, R. (1983). *Political judgment.* Chicago: University of Chicago Press.

Bellah, R., Madsen, R., Sullivan, W., Swidler, A., & Tipton, S. (1985). *Habits of the heart: Individualism and commitment in American life.* Berkeley: University of California Press.

Bellow, G., & Kettleson, J. (1978). From ethics to politics: Confronting scarcity and fairness in public interest practice. *Boston University Law Review, 58,* 337.

Benveniste, G. (1987). *Professionalizing the organization: Reducing bureaucracy to enhance effectiveness.* San Francisco: Jossey-Bass.

Berliner, D. C. (1986). In pursuit of the expert pedagogue. *Educational Researcher, 15* (7), 5–13.

Berman, M. (1982). *All that is solid melts into air.* New York: Simon & Schuster.

Bernstein, R. J. (1983). *Beyond objectivism and relativism.* Philadelphia: University of Pennsylvania Press.

Beyer, L. E. (1984). Field experience, ideology, and the development of critical reflectivity. *Journal of Teacher Education, 35* (3), 36–41.

Beyer, L. E. (1988a). *Knowing and acting: Inquiry, ideology and educational studies.* London: Falmer Press.

Beyer, L. E. (1988b). Training and educating: A critique of technical-mindedness in teacher preparation. *Current Issues in Education, VIII*, 21–40.

Beyer, L. E. (1989). Reconceptualizing teacher preparation: Institutions and ideologies. *Journal of Teacher Education, 40* (1), 22–26.

Beyer, L. E., & Apple, M. W. (Eds.). (1988). *The curriculum: Problems, politics, and possibilities*. Albany: State University of New York Press.

Beyer, L. E., & Zeichner, K. M. (1987). Teacher education in cultural context: Beyond reproduction. In T. S. Popkewitz (Ed.), *Critical studies in teacher education: Its folklore, theory and practice* (pp. 298–334). London: Falmer Press.

Bledstein, B. J. (1976). *The culture of professionalism: The middle class and the development of higher education in America*. New York: Norton.

Bleier, R. (1984). *Science and gender: A critique of biology and its theories on women*. New York: Pergamon.

Bloom, A. (1987). *The closing of the American mind*. New York: Simon & Schuster.

Boisjoly, R. (1988, March). "Whistle-blower." *Life, 11* (3), 3, 17, 20, 22.

Borrowman, M. L. (1956). *The liberal and technical in teacher education*. New York: Bureau of Publications, Teachers College.

Boyer, E. L. (1983). *High school: A report on secondary education in America*. New York: Harper & Row.

Bursztajn, H., Feinbloom, R. I., Hamm, R. M., & Brodsky, A. (1981). *Medical choices, medical chances*. New York: Delacorte.

Cain, M. (1983). The general practice lawyer and the client: Towards a radical conception. In R. Dingwall & P. Lewis (Eds.), *The sociology of the professions: Lawyers, doctors and others* (pp. 106–130). New York: St. Martins.

Carnegie Forum on Education and the Economy. (1986). *A nation prepared: Teachers for the 21st century*. New York: Author.

Case, C. W., Lanier, J. E., & Miskel, C. G. (1986). The Holmes Group report: Impetus for gaining professional status for teachers. *Journal of Teacher Education, 37* (4), 36–43.

Cassell, E. J. (1976). *The healers art: A new approach to doctor-patient relationships*. Philadelphia: Lippincott.

Cavell, S. (1979). *The claim of reason*. Oxford: Oxford University Press.

Clandinin, D. J. (1986). *Classroom practice: Teacher images in action*. London: Falmer Press.

Clark, B. (1987). *The academic profession: National, disciplinary, and institutional settings*. Berkeley: University of California Press.

Clifford, G. J., & Guthrie, J. W. (1988). *Ed school: A brief for professional education*. Chicago: University of Chicago Press.

Collins, R. (1979). *The credential society: An historical sociology of education and stratification*. Orlando, FL: Academic Press.

Cremin, L. A. (1957). *The republic and the school: Horace Mann on the education of free men*. New York: Teachers College Press.

Culler, J. (1982). *On deconstruction: Theory and criticism after structuralism*. Ithaca, NY: Cornell University Press.

Davis, M. H. (1981). Critical jurisprudence: An essay on the legal theory of Robert Burt's taking care of strangers. *Wisconsin Law Review*, 419–453.

DeLoughry, T. J. (1988a, July 20). Engineering students are said to get incoherent education in the liberal arts. *Chronicle of Higher Education*, pp. 1, 14–15.

DeLoughry, T. J. (1988b, February 24). Failure of colleges to teach computer ethics is called oversight with potentially catastrophic consequences. *Chronicle of Higher Education*, pp. A15, A18.

Derrida, J. (1976). *Of grammatology*. Baltimore, MD: Johns Hopkins University Press.

Dewey, J. (1916). *Democracy and education*. New York: Macmillan.

Douglass, F. (1982). *Narrative of the life of Frederick Douglass, an American slave*. New York: Penguin. (Original work published 1845)

Du Bois, B. (1983). Passionate scholarship: Notes on values, knowing and method. In G. Bowles & R. D. Klein (Eds.), *Theories of women's studies* (pp. 105–116). Boston: Routledge & Kegan Paul.

Edwards, R. (1979). *Contested terrain*. New York: Basic Books.

Eigo, F. A. (Ed.). (1986). *The professions in ethical context: Vocations to justice and love*. Villanova, PA: Villanova University Press.

Elsbree, W. S. (1939). *The American teacher: Evolution of a profession in a democracy*. New York: American Book Company.

Enthoven, A. C. (1980). *Health plan*. Reading, MA: Addison-Wesley.

Enthoven, A. C. (1982). *Competition and market forces: An answer to cost containment in health care*. Paper presented to the Faculty Seminar in Medicine and Society, University of Illinois at Urbana-Champaign.

Etzioni, A. (1969). *The semi-professions and their organization*. New York: Free Press.

Feinberg, W. (1983). *Understanding education*. New York: Cambridge University Press.

Feinberg, W. (1987). The Holmes Group report and the professionalization of teaching. *Teachers College Record*, *88* (3), 366–377.

Fenstermacher, G. (1986). Philosophy of research on teaching: Three aspects. In M. C. Wittrock (Ed.), *Handbook of research on teaching* (pp. 37–49). New York: Macmillan.

Fiss, O. (1985). (Open correspondence with P. D. Carrington). In P. W. Martin, "Of Law and the River," and of Nihilism and Academic Freedom. *Journal of Legal Education*, *35*, 1–26.

Floden, R. E., & Clark, C. M. (1988). Preparing teachers for uncertainty. *Teachers College Record*, *89* (4), 505–524.

Foster, J. C. (1986). *The ideology of apolitical politics: The elite lawyer's response to the legitimation crisis in American capitalism: 1870–1920.* Millwood, NY: Associated Faculty Press.

Fox, R. C. (1957). Training for uncertainty. In R. K. Merton, G. G. Reader, & P. Kendall (Eds.), *The student physician* (pp. 207–241). Cambridge, MA: Harvard University Press.

Freud, S. (1930). *Civilization and its discontents* (J. Strachey, Trans.). New York: Norton.

Gadamer, H.-G. (1982). *Truth and method* (G. Barden & J. Cumming, Eds. and Trans.). New York: Crossroad.

Gadamer, H.-G. (1987). The problem of historical consciousness. In R. Rabinow & W. M. Sullivan (Eds.), *Interpretive social science, A second look* (pp. 82–140). Berkeley: University of California Press.

Gallop, J. (1985). *The daughter's seduction.* Ithaca, NY: Cornell University Press.

Geertz, C. (1973). *The interpretation of culture.* New York: Harper & Row.

Glazer, N. (1974). The schools of the minor professions. *Minerva, 12* (3), 346–364.

Goldman, A. H. (1980). *The moral foundations of professional ethics.* Totowa, NJ: Rowan & Littlefield.

Goode, W. J. (1962). The librarian: From occupation to profession? In P. H. Ennis & H. W. Winger (Eds.), *Seven questions about the profession of librarianship* (pp. 8–22). Chicago: University of Chicago Press.

Goodlad, J. I. (1984). *A place called school.* New York: McGraw-Hill.

Goodman, J. (1986). Teaching preservice teachers a critical approach to curriculum design: A descriptive account. *Curriculum Inquiry, 16* (2), 181–201.

Gowin, D. B. (1981). *Educating.* Ithaca, NY: Cornell University Press.

Graff, G. (1987). *Professing literature: An institutional history.* Chicago: University of Chicago Press.

Greene, J. C. (1981). *Science, ideology, and world view.* Berkeley: University of California Press.

Greene, M. (1978). *Landscapes of learning.* New York: Teachers College Press.

Grumet, M. (June, 1988). *On daffodils that come before the swallows dare.* Paper presented at the Stanford University Conference on Qualitative Research, Stanford, CA.

Grundy, S. (1987). *Curriculum: Product or praxis?* London: Falmer Press.

Habermas, J. (1971). *Knowledge and human interests* (J. J. Shapiro, Trans.). Boston: Beacon Press.

Habermas, J. (1979). *Communication and the evolution of society* (T. McCarthy, Ed. and Trans.). Boston: Beacon Press.

Habermas, J. (1984). *The theory of communicative action: Vol. 1. Reason and the rationalization of society* (T. McCarthy, Ed. and Trans.). Boston: Beacon Press.

Hamerow, T. S. (1987). *Reflections on history and historians.* Madison: University of Wisconsin Press.

Harding, S. (1986). *The science question in feminism.* Ithaca, NY: Cornell University Press.

Harper, C. A. (1939). *A century of public teacher education.* Washington, DC: National Education Association.

Harris, J. E. (1977). The internal organization of hospitals: Some economic implications. *Bell Journal of Economics, 8* (2), 467–482.

Haskell, T. L. (1984). Professionalism versus capitalism: R. H. Tawney, Emile Durkheim and C. S. Peirce on the disinterestedness of professional communities. In T. L. Haskell (Ed.), *The authority of experts* (pp. 180–225). Bloomington: Indiana University Press.

Heinz, J. P. (1983). The power of lawyers. *Georgia Law Review, 17* (4), 891–911.

Heinz, J. P., & Laumann, E. O. (1982). *Chicago lawyers: The social structure of the bar.* New York: Russell Sage Foundation and American Bar Association.

Hirsch, E. D. (1987). *Cultural literacy: What every American needs to know.* Boston: Houghton Mifflin.

Hoffman, N. (1981). *Woman's "true" profession: Voices from the history of teaching.* Old Westbury, NY: The Feminist Press.

Holmes Group. (1986). *Tomorrow's teachers: A report of the Holmes Group.* East Lansing, MI: Author.

Holt, M. (1987). *Judgment, planning, and educational change.* New York: Harper & Row.

Homans, G. C. (1982). The relevance of psychology to the explanation of social phenomena. In E. Bredo & W. Feinberg (Eds.), *Knowledge and values in social and educational research* (pp. 53–69). Philadelphia: Temple University Press.

Hosticka, C. (1979). We don't care what happened, we only care about what is going to happen: Lawyer-client negotiations of reality. *Social Problems, 26* (5), 599–610.

Hughes, E. (1959). The study of occupations. In R. K. Merton, L. Broom, & L. S. Cottrell, Jr. (Eds.), *Sociology today* (pp. 442–458). New York: Basic Books.

Hughes, E. C. (1963). Professions. *Daedalus, 92* (4), 655–668.

Illich, I. (1980). *Toward a history of needs.* New York: Bantam.

Irigaray, L. (1985). *Speculum of the other woman.* Ithaca, NY: Cornell University Press.

Israel, L. (1982). *Decision-making: The modern doctor's dilemma.* New York: Random House.

Jackson, P. W. (1968). *Life in classrooms.* New York: Holt, Rinehart & Winston.

Jackson, P. W. (1987). Facing our ignorance. *Teachers College Reocrd, 88* (3), 384–441.

Johnston, J. S., Zemsky, R., & Shaman, S. (1988). *Unfinished design: The humanities and social sciences in undergraduate engineering education.* Washington, DC: Association of American Colleges.

Jonsen, A. R., & Jameton, A. L. (1977). Social and political responsibilities of physicians. *Journal of Medicine and Philosophy, 2* (4), 376–400.

Keller, E. F. (1983). *A feeling for the organism: The life and work of Barbara McClintock.* New York: Freeman.

Keller, E. F. (1985). *Reflections on gender and science.* New Haven, CT: Yale University Press.

Kozol, J. (1986). *The night is dark and I am far from home.* New York: Continuum.

Kultgen, J. (1988). *Ethics and professionalism.* Philadelphia: University of Pennsylvania Press.

Lacan, J. (1985). *Feminine sexuality.* New York: Norton.

Laird, S. (1987, April). *Betsey Brown vs. philosophy of education? A case study of "maternal teaching."* Paper presented at the annual meeting of the American Educational Research Association, Washington, DC.

Laird, S. (1988, June). *Reclaiming a conversation at Cornell College: A case study of curricular transformation in liberal education, teacher education, and women's studies.* Paper presented to the annual meeting of the National Women's Studies Association, Minneapolis, MN.

Larson, M. S. (1977). *The rise of professionalism: A sociological analysis.* Berkeley: University of California Press.

Lasch, C. (1984). *The minimal self.* New York: Norton.

Levinson, S. (1970). On "Teaching" Political "Science." In P. Green & S. Levinson, (Eds.), *Power and community: Dissenting essays in political science* (pp. 59–84). New York: Vintage.

Levinson, S. (1988). *Constitutional faith.* Princeton, NJ: Princeton University Press.

Light, D., Jr. (1979). Uncertainty and control in professional training. *Journal of Health and Social Behavior, 20* (4), 310–322.

Lightfoot, S. L. (1983). *The good high school: Portraits of character and culture.* New York: Basic Books.

Linowitz, S. (1988, September 14). Law schools must help make the practice of law the learned and humane profession it once was. *Chronicle of Higher Education,* p. A52.

Liston, D. P., & Zeichner, K. M. (1987). Reflective teacher education and moral deliberation. *Journal of Teacher Education, 38* (6), 2–8.

Lortie, D. C. (1969). The balance of control and autonomy in elementary school teaching. In A. Etzioni (Ed.), *The semi-professions and their organization: Teachers, nurses, social workers* (pp. 1–53). New York: Free Press.

Lortie, D. C. (1975). *Schoolteacher.* Chicago: University of Chicago Press.

MacIntyre, A. (1984). *After virtue: A study in moral theory* (2nd ed.). Notre Dame, IN: University of Notre Dame Press.

MacIntyre, A. (1988). *Whose justice? which rationality?* Notre Dame, IN: University of Notre Dame Press.

Macaulay, S. (1987). Images of law in everyday life: The lessons of school, entertainment, and spectator sports. *Law and Society Review, 21* (2), 185–218.

Marmor, T. (1973). *The politics of Medicare* (rev. Am. ed.). Chicago: Aldine.

Marsh, P. T. (1988). *Contesting the boundaries of liberal and professional education: The Syracuse experiment.* Syracuse, NY: Syracuse University Press.

Martin, J. R. (1985). *Reclaiming a conversation: The ideal of the educated woman.* New Haven, CT: Yale University Press.

Marx, K. (1967). *The communist manifesto* (S. Moore, Trans.). New York: Penguin. (Original work published 1848).

Mason, J. K. (1988). *Human life and medical practice.* Edinburgh: Edinburgh University Press.

Mattingly, P. H. (1975). *The classless profession: American schoolmen in the nineteenth century.* New York: New York University Press.

McCarthy, T. (1978). *The critical theory of Jürgen Habermas.* Cambridge, MA: MIT Press.

McCurdy, J. (1988, April 27). Bennett calls Stanford's curriculum revision "Capitulation" to Pressure. *Chronicle of Higher Education,* p. 2.

McWilliams, W. C. (1970). Political arts and political sciences. In P. Green & S. Levinson (Eds.), *Power and community: Dissenting essays in political science,* (pp. 357–382). New York: Vintage.

Metzger, W. R. (1987). A spectre haunts American scholars: The spectre of "Professionism." *Educational Researcher, 16* (6), 10–18.

Mooney, C. J. (1988, December 14). Sweeping curricular change is underway at Stanford as university phases out its "Western culture" program. *Chronicle of Higher Education,* pp. A1, A11–13.

Morawetz, T. (1978). *Wittgenstein and knowledge.* Boston: University of Massachusetts Press.

Nasaw, D. (1979). *Schooled to order: A social history of public schooling in the United States.* Oxford: Oxford University Press.

National Commission on Excellence in Education. (1983). *A nation at risk: The imperative for educational reform.* Washington, DC: U.S. Government Printing Office.

National Commission for Excellence in Teacher Education. (1985). *A call for change in teacher education.* Washington, DC: American Association of Colleges for Teacher Education.

Nelson, R. L. (1988). *Partners with power: Social transformation of the large law firm.* Berkeley: University of California Press.

Newman, J. H. (1976). *The idea of a university defined and illustrated.* Oxford: Clarendon Press. (Original work published 1852)

Noble, D. (1984). *Forces of production: A social history of industrial automation.* New York: Knopf.

Noddings, N. (1984). *Caring: A feminine approach to ethics and moral education.* Berkeley: University of California Press.

Nyberg, D. & Egan, K. (1984). *The erosion of education.* New York: Teachers College Press.

Page, D. P. (1847). *Theory and practice of teaching: Or, the motives and methods of good school-keeping.* Syracuse, NY: Hall & Dickson.

Parsons, T. (1937). Remarks on education and the professions. *International Journal of Ethics, 47* (3), 365–369.

Parsons, T. (1951). *The social system.* New York: Free Press.

Parsons, T. (1954). *Essays in sociological theory* (rev. ed.). Glencoe, IL: Free Press.

Parsons, T. (1959). The school class as a social system: Some of its functions in American society. *Harvard Educational Review, 29* (4), 297–318.

Parsons, T. (1962). The law and social control. In W. M. Evans (Ed.), *Law and sociology* (pp. 65–78). New York: Free Press.

Parsons, T. (1968). Professions. In D. L. Sills (Ed.), *International encyclopedia of the social sciences* (Vol. 12, pp. 536–547). New York: Macmillan and Free Press.

Parsons, T., & Bales, R. F. (1955). *Family, socialization and interaction process.* New York: Free Press.

Parsons, T., Bales, R. F., & Shils, E. A. (1953). *Working papers in the theory of action.* Glencoe, IL: Free Press.

Parsons, T., & Platt, G. M. (1973). *The American university.* Cambridge, MA: Harvard University Press.

Petrie, H. G. (1987). Teacher education, the liberal arts, and extended education programs. *Educational Policy, 1* (1), 29–41.

Piven, F., & Cloward, R. (1971). *Regulating the poor.* New York: Pantheon.

Plato (1980). The laws. In T. Pangle (Trans.), *The laws of Plato.* New York: Basic Books.

Reiser, S. J. (1978). *Medicine and the reign of technology.* Cambridge: Cambrige University Press.

Richardson, L. (1900). *The normal school idea.* Albany, NY: J. B. Lyon.

Rorty, R. (1979). *Philosophy and the mirror of nature.* Princeton, NJ: Princeton University Press.

Rousseau, J. J. (1979). *Emile* (A. Bloom, Trans.). New York: Basic Books. (Original work published 1762)

Rueschemeyer, D. (1964). Doctors and lawyers: A comment on the theory of the professions. *Canadian Review of Sociology and Anthropology, 1* (1), 17–30.

Rugg, H. (1952). *The teacher of teachers: Frontiers of theory and practice in teacher education.* New York: Harper & Brothers.

Ryle, G. (1949). *The concept of mind.* New York: Harper & Row.

Sarat, A., & Felstiner, W. L. F. (1986). Law and strategy in the divorce lawyer's office. *Law and Society Review, 20* (1), 93–134.

Schaffer, T. L. (1987). *Faith and the professions.* Provo, UT: Brigham Young University.

Schön, D. A. (1983). *The reflective practitioner: How professionals think in action.* New York: Basic Books.

Schön, D. A. (1987). *Educating the reflective practitioner.* San Francisco: Jossey-Bass.

Shannon, P. (1989). *Broken promises: Reading instruction in twentieth-century America.* Granby, MA: Bergin & Garvey.

Shulman, L. S. (1987). Knowledge and teaching: Foundations of the new reform. *Harvard Educational Review, 57* (1), 1–22.

Simon, W. H. (1978). The ideology of advocacy: Procedural justice and professional ethics. *Wisconsin Law Review,* 29–144.

Simon, W. H. (1980). Homo psychologicus: Notes on a new legal formalism. *Stanford Law Review, 32,* 487–559.

Simon, W. H. (1984). Visions of Practice in Legal Thought. *Stanford Law Review, 36* (1 & 2), 469–507.

Sizer, T. R. (1984). *Horace's compromise: The dilemma of the American high school.* Boston: Houghton Mifflin.

Smigel, E. (1969). *The Wall Street lawyer: Professional organization man?* (2nd ed.). Bloomington: Indiana University Press.

Smith, J. H. (1988). *The spirit and its letter: Traces of rhetoric in Hegel's philosophy of Bildung.* Ithaca, NY: Cornell University Press.

Snyder, A. (1972). *Dauntless women in childhood education 1856–1931.* Washington, DC: Association for Childhood Education International.

Southern Regional Education Board (n.d.). *Improving teacher education: An agenda for higher education and the schools.* Atlanta, GA: Southern Regional Education Board.

Stark, J. S., & Lowther, M. A. (1988). *Strengthening the ties that bind: Integrating undergraduate liberal and professional study.* Ann Arbor: University of Michigan.

Starr, P. (1982). *The social transformation of American medicine.* New York: Basic Books.

Sternberg, R. J. (1986). Introduction: The nature and scope of practical intelligence. In R. J. Sternberg & R. K. Wagner (Eds.), *Practical intelligence: Nature and origins of competence in the everyday world* (pp. 1–10). Cambridge: Cambridge University Press.

Sykes, G. (1987). Reckoning with the spector. *Educational Researcher, 16* (6), 19–21.

Taylor, C. (1985). *Philosophical papers: Vol. 1. Human agency and language.* Cambridge: Cambridge University Press.

Tom, A. R. (1987). A critique of the rationale for extended teacher preparation. *Educational Policy, 1* (1), 43–56.

Toulmin, S. (1972). *Human understanding: The collective use and evolution of concepts.* Princeton, NJ: Princeton University Press.

University of Michigan. (1986). Law school announcement 1986–87. *University of Michigan Bulletin, 15* (13), 14–15.

Vallance, E. (1977). Hiding the hidden curriculum: An interpretation of the language of justification in nineteenth-century educational reform. In A. A. Bellack & H. M. Kliebard (Eds.), *Curriculum and evaluation* (pp. 590–607). Berkeley, CA: McCutchan.

Veatch, R. M. (1987). *The patient as partner: A theory of human-experimental ethics.* Bloomington: Indiana University Press.

Vild, K. A. (1984). The civil engineering degree: Education or training? *Journal of Professional Issues in Engineering, 110* (1), 25–30.

Walsh, D. C. (1987). *Corporate physicians: Between medicine and management.* New Haven, CT: Yale University Press.

Weinsheimer, J. C. (1985). *Gadamer's hermeneutics: A reading of truth and method.* New Haven, CT: Yale University Press.

Williams, R. (1977). *Marxism and literature.* Oxford: Oxford University Press.

Willis, P. (1981). *Learning to labor: How working class kids get working class jobs.* New York: Columbia University Press.

Wittgenstein, L. (1968). *Philosophical investigations* (G. E. M. Anscombe, Trans.). New York: Macmillan. (Original work published 1953)

Wood, G. H. (1984). Schooling in a democracy: Transformation or reproduction? *Educational Theory, 34* (3), 219–239.

Young, E. F. (1901). *Isolation in the school.* Chicago: University of Chicago Press.

Zeichner, K. M. (1980). Myths and realities: Field based experiences in preservice teacher education. *Journal of Teacher Education, 31* (3), 45–55.

Index

About the Authors

Landon E. Beyer is Chair of the Department of Education at Knox College. He holds an M.A. in philosophy and a Ph.D. in education, both from the University of Wisconsin—Madison. His recent publications include *Knowing and Acting: Inquiry, Ideology, and Educational Studies* (The Falmer Press, 1988); *The Curriculum: Problems, Politics, and Possibilities* (State University of New York Press, 1988); and *Critical Reflection and the Culture of Schooling: Empowering Teachers* (Deakin University Press, 1989).

Walter Feinberg, who received his Ph.D. in philosophy from Boston University, is currently Professor of Philosophy of Education and Educational Policy Studies at the University of Illinois at Urbana-Champaign. His recent publications include *Knowledge and Values in Social and Educational Research* (Temple University Press, 1982); *Understanding Education* (Cambridge University Press, 1983); and *School and Society* (Teachers College Press, 1985).

Jo Anne Pagano teaches in the Department of Education and in Women's Studies at Colgate University; her research focuses on feminist theory, the philosophy of education, and curriculum studies. She received a Ph.D. in education from the University of Rochester. Her book *Exiles and Communities: Teaching in the Patriarchical Wilderness* will be published by the State University of New York Press in 1990.

Tony Whitson is currently an Assistant Professor in the Department of Curriculum and Instruction at Louisiana State University. He received his A.B. from Harvard University and J.D. from the University of Wisconsin—Madison, after which he practiced as a public interest lawyer. He received his Ph.D. in education at the University of Rochester. His book, *Constitution and Curriculum: Hermeneutical Semiotics of Cases and Controversies in Education, Law, and Social Science*, will be published by the Falmer Press in 1989.